FOR PEACE
VOICES OF DESPAIR AND HOPE THROUGH THE AGES

An anthology edited by

Ruth Finnegan

THE SEARCH FOR PEACE

callender press

ISBN 978-1-4466-5986-1
2023

Callender Press
www.callenderpress.co.uk

"Yesterday is gone. Tomorrow has not yet come. We have only today".
Mother Teresa

Contents

Contents
5

Preface
9

VOICES OF PEACE
14

From the Vedic scriptures
14

The lion and the lamb
17

"Let all this be a thing of the past"
19

The pain of war
21

"Peace is the beauty of life"
26

The Town Mouse and the Country Mouse
30

War and Peace in the Qur'an
32

Dulce bellum inexpertis
35

Hymns, songs and blessings
39

An Exhortation to Peace and Unity
46

Quaker witnesses over the centuries: Peace affirming and its dilemmas
52

The War Prayer
60

The way of peace
64

The eternal reciprocity of tears
69

War at any price?
81

Manifesto
91

Pacem in terris—Peace on Earth
94

The quest for peace and justice
101

The beginning of peace is love
113

The peace and the necessity of truth and reconciliation
119

The bitter legacy of war
125

Afghanistan
125

Syria
126

Ukraine
128

Russia
131

X
131

Gaza 2023
132

The victims, the inspirers
132

Hiroshima
135

A FEW PEACE
141

SYMBOLS
141

*****
144

FURTHER THOUGHTS
146

Preface

This book began in homage and love for my brave father, Tom Finnegan, who died, too young, in 1964. It expanded as I found more and more fine writers on peace; I had no idea until I found myself in their midst that there were so many, and from every age and background and clime.

I am reminded of this daily as I look at the portrait of Erasmus, that inspired speaker for peace, now hanging on my study wall as it once did on my father's. I found myself immersed in the variegated and great voices from throughout the world and the centuries — and then going on to the others reproduced in this collection.

I hope it will serve as an introduction to the wonderful body of courageous speakers for peace, blessedly too large to be more than lightly sampled here.

The central tenets here are most often, given my own background, from Christianity. Some however are drawn, as they must be, from the rich insights of other traditions. They are essential in throwing light on the parallelisms between the great faiths in their search for peace and reconciliation among all peoples, in our day, in the past, and, we would hope, in the future.

For who, from the far mists of time up to the generations of today, is *not* interested in peace?

Not all peace-seekers have taken the same approach, however, or see peace in the same light, for searchers for peace come in many different colours. Sometimes peace is conceived as something positive, spiritual, whether at individual or community or, indeed, world level; sometimes merely more as just the absence of war and conflict, an ample reward in itself - "Better beans and bacon in peace than cakes and ale in fear", as Aesop's country mouse had it (we will hear more of him in due course).

Some seekers are contemplatives: poets, prophets, singers; some see peace as a thing of the individual soul, springing from the world of the spirit rather than from the social order; others again are predominantly pragmatists and people of action. Some speak in prose – sermons, books, exhortations - and at length; others in verse or song or in small gems of wisdom; others again in pictorial images or artefacts. Some speak to the world; others to God, under whatever name; some for themselves only. Some voices come from the very heat of battle or the agony of destruction and massacre, others dwell on emotion or

thought in tranquility. Some seek the pure way of peace whatever the conditions, idealists ever; others hold that for peace to flourish justice and truth must be there too. Others act through small gifts of generosity, like the grant of land to Syrian settlers in Gaza, on the face of it nothing to do with peace yet intrinsic to it; others with potent imagery like the Arabic proverb's "seed" or Mother Teresa's "smile", the beginning, as she tells it, of peace.

Then there are those who draw on ancient wisdom, such as Adamnan's thoughtful "Law of the innocents" in seventh-century Ireland, drawn up to safeguard non-combatants in time of conflict. Then too, following in his footsteps and those of early Muslim and Hindu thinkers, there are the down-to-earth and influential *Geneva Conventions* (not included here as readily available, though alas too often flouted). These drew their inspiration from many thinkers and activists through centuries, further spurred into action by the Swiss businessman Henry Dunant, after, shocked, seeing wounded soldiers abandoned to linger and die after the battle of Solferino in 1859.

Over the years these conventions have gone through a series of evolving and carefully negotiated forms, agreed by many nations. They work to protect not only prisoners, hostages, and the wounded, but also, in a sequence of detailed and carefully crafted clauses, medical and religious personnel together with medical units and transport in time of armed conflict. As we know too well, they are not always followed.

Amidst this the idealists and poets and philosophers are sorely needed too—it is only too easy to slip from the intended way if we are not constantly reminded - and reminded too in words and images that are both heartfelt and beautiful, like many included here. But the practical institutional applications are of the essence too. They have gone some way to save people from the worst horrors of war - " people", remember, means men, women, children: living, feeling suffering human beings like you and me (how often do the commanders in their weapon-proof bastions remember that?). They have indeed done much toward restoring the ways of reconciliation and peace that all, surely all, must long for.

This is not a book to be read all the way through at sitting. Rather it is a selection of insights, short and long, to be dipped into as inclination allows or as the days roll past – a source and resource book that I hope will be illuminating for readers of all kinds.

All the world is here in its many centuries of human struggle.

Like all editors, I have many thanks to offer. In particular I would thank

Abdullah Mohammed for insights into, and quotations from, the *Qur'an*, George Weigel for drawing attention to that all too perceptive term "the fog of war", Malachy O'Neill for sending me the Irish Great War poem which I would never have discovered otherwise, Eamonn OCiardha for directing me to Adamnan's "Law of the innocents, and Jim Graham for continued inspiration and criticism; also, and above all, to the often anonymous and untraceable poets of recent wars, some no longer living, who have been prepared to share their insights, griefs and endurance on the internet and whom I have taken the liberty of reproducing here—all glory to them. I think they would wish their voices to be heard.

Most of the extracts here are either long out of print or, where not already in one way or another in the public domain (as with the contemporary war poems by often anonymous authors on the internet), have been cleared with their rights holders. I have done my best to find and contact all relevant copyright holders but would be grateful for any information about unacknowledged rights holders of any of the items reproduced here: please contact me so I can make amends.

Near-finally, let me thank my mother, practical as well as peace-making - long dead but constantly recalled by those who knew her.

Last and best of all, let me dedicate this collection to the youth of today. For peace or for war, the future of our precious and beautiful world lies in your hands.

Ruth

Shenley Wood, Milton Keynes
amidst the gold autumn trees 2023

VOICES OF PEACE

From the Vedic scriptures[1]
The ancient and present voice of Hinduism

References to peace and its implications are, as with the Koran, scattered through the verses of the ancient Indian scripture rather than integrated in one place. These insights from the extensive Vedic literature represent what is probably the oldest tradition of knowledge in the world, still in evidence today.

This is peace in a different sense from some of the other extracts and yet not unrelated. It is peace as an inner meditative state, an awareness of being one with the universe in an eternity outside time and the ephemeral sufferings of the mundane world – to be able (in a lovely image) to "pluck the strings of your inner soul."

Passive all this might seem and in one sense that is so – inward looking, dwelling on personal spiritual experience and individual happiness rather than outward action. And yet – there is also the injunction not to regard oneself as separate from others in the universe but

"A part and parcel of Universal Joy",

"None is our enemy",

> *"May we resolve to dedicate our life*
> *to the service of humankind,*
> *and uplift them to Divinity"*
> *and*
> *"Peace be everywhere,*
> *Peace, only peace,*
> *Peace be in my mind and heart".*

The one who loves all intensely
begins perceiving in all living beings
a part of himself.
He becomes a lover of all,
a part and parcel of the Universal Joy.

---

[1] Sources: primarily from http://chaplaincyinstitute.org/library/blessings-and-prayers/quotes-ancient-scriptures-of-hinduism/, and http://yogaindailylife.org.au/blog/2013/06/20/vedic-mantras-for-world-peace-1and http://www.aryasamaj.com/enews/2010/oct/2.htm/ (accessed April-May 2017).

14

He flows with the stream of happiness,
and is enriched by each soul.

Yajur Veda

Sing the song of celestial love, O singer!
May the divine fountain of eternal grace and joy
enter your soul.
May Brahma, (the Divine One),
Pluck the strings of your inner soul
with His celestial fingers,
And feel His own presence within.
Bless us with a divine voice
That we may tune the harp-strings of our life
To sing songs of Love to you.

Rig Veda

O Almighty!
You are the infinite; the universe is also infinite!
From infinite the infinite has come out!
Having taken infinite out of the infinite, the infinite remains!
O Almighty! May there be Peace! Peace! Everywhere!

Ishawashya Upanishad

O seeker, know the true nature of your soul,
and identify yourself with it completely.
O Lord, (may we attain) the everlasting consciousness
of Supreme Light and Joy.
May we resolve to dedicate our life
to the service of humankind,
and uplift them to Divinity.

Yajur Veda

Bright but hidden, the Self dwells in the heart.
Everything that moves, breathes, opens, and closes
Lives in the Self. He is the source of love
And may be known through love but not through thought
He is the goal of life. Attain this goal!

Mundaka Upanishad

All is change in the world of the senses,
But changeless is the supreme Lord of Love.
Meditate on him, be absorbed by him,
Wake up from this dream of separateness.

Shvetashvatara Upanishad

Lead us from unreality to reality.

Lead us from darkness to light.
Lead us from death to immortality.
May everyone be healthy.
May everyone live in peace.
May the wishes of everyone be fulfilled.
May everyone attain perfection.
May there be happiness and prosperity everywhere.

Peace be in the universe,
Peace be in the atmosphere,
Peace be on earth,
Peace be in the waters,
Peace be in the herbs,
Peace be in the vegetation,
Peace be in the elements,
Peace of the Supreme,

Peace be everywhere,
Peace, only peace,
Peace be in my mind and heart

Brhadaranyaka Upanishad

Blessed are the eyes that cast the affectionate glances at others.
All are our friends, none is our enemy.
Love begets love and hatred breeds poison and contempt

Atharva Veda

I am not in one but I am in millions.
I have millions of eyes, ears and lives.
They are I and I am They.

Atharva Veda

16

The lion and the lamb[2]
The Prophet Isaiah

These famous verses were written in Israel, in Hebrew, probably sometime in the eighth to seventh centuries BC. They have been a source of inspiration for millennia not only the age-old seekers for peace but also for painters and the present-day environmental movement.

The wolf will live with the lamb,
the leopard will lie down with the goat,

the calf and the lion and the yearling together;
and a little child will lead them.

The cow will feed with the bear,
their young will lie down together, and the lion will eat straw like the ox.

The infant will play near the cobra's den,
and the young child will put its hand into the viper's nest.

They will neither harm nor destroy
on all my holy mountain,

for the earth will be filled with the knowledge of the LORD
as the waters cover the sea.

---

[2] Source: *The Old Testament, Book of Isaiah* chapter 11, verses 6-9 (New International translation).

Andrew Murray The lion lies down with the lamb

"Let all this be a thing of the past"[3]
Homer

No one knows for sure when or where the great poet Homer lived, whether he was, as legend has it, in fact blind (surely he had the more important sight, the spiritual) or indeed whether he was really several people, or even perhaps a woman. Most likely it was sometime around the seventh or eighth century BC (but no doubt, in its oral roots, earlier), and in Greece. Almost certainly the lays were orally inspired and delivered, and in at least some sense improvised, certainly sung for an audience and to a lyre.

Whatever the background his epics, the Iliad *and* Odyssey, *now written down, plentifully translated and recognised as among the greatest literary works of all time, have influenced, shaped and inspired from that day to this and throughout the world.*

The Iliad *tells the story of the siege of Troy in mythic times by an alliance of Greek forces. As such it might be assumed that in this most war-suffused of all military epics it would be dominated by the glory of battle, the triumph of slaughter. And indeed, there is much celebration of heroism and of the drama of war. This is central for example in this stirring and rightly famous passage*

"The two forces met with a fearful din of spears and bossed shields, clashing in a fierce and furious mêlée of bronze-breasted fighters. And there the screams of the dying were mingled with cries of triumph and blood flowed over the earth. As when two winter torrents flow down from great mountain springs to mingle their turbulent floods; where the two streams meet and thunder on down a deep gorge, and the shepherd far off in the mountains hears the roar, so now as the two armies clashed in the fury of battle a terrible roar of toil and shouting arose".

No one could call the Iliad *a pacifist work. And yet—running through is a vein of compassion that shines the more brightly for its military setting. Can there be anything more deeply infused with compassion, the most moving perhaps of all literature, than when the hero Achilles, the war-maddened slayer of Priam's son Hector, weeps together with Priam, who has come a suppliant to beg for his son's body for burial—a prayer, not a demand. They are weeping for the pity of war and its sorrows and its human loss, until, deeply moved, Achilles grants Priam's prayer, and sends him away with the body of his son and much respect.*

Thousands have wept with them through the centuries.

---

[3] Source: selected verses from Homer's *Iliad* and *Odyssey* (various translators).

I wish that strife would vanish away from among gods and mortals, and gall, which makes a man grow angry for all his great mind, that gall of anger that swarms like smoke inside of a man's heart and becomes a thing sweeter to him by far than the dripping of honey.

Ah my friend, if you and I could escape this fray and live forever, never a trace of age, immortal, I would never fight on the front lines again or command you to the field where men win fame.

Like the generations of leaves, the lives of mortal men. Now the wind scatters the old leaves across the earth, now the living timber bursts with the new buds and spring comes round again. And so with men: as one generation comes to life, another dies away.

There can be no covenants between men and lions, wolves and lambs can never be of one mind, but hate each other out and out and through. Therefore there can be no understanding between you and me, nor may there be any covenants between us, till one or other shall fall.

Ruin, eldest daughter of Zeus, she blinds us all, that fatal madness—she with those delicate feet of hers, never touching the earth, gliding over the heads of men to trap us all. She entangles one man, now another.

We are perpetually labouring to destroy our delights, our composure, our devotion to superior power. Of all the animals on earth we least know what is good for us.

Still, we will let all this be a thing of the past, though it hurts us, and beat down by constraint the anger that rises inside us. Now I am making an end of my anger. It does not become me, unrelentingly to rage on.

What are the children of men, but as leaves that drop at the wind's breath?
When spring season comes again, the budding wood grows up.
And so with men: one generation grows, another dies away.

Of all creatures that breathe and move on earth none is more to be pitied than a man.

There have been lyrists for centuries (as in this Mesopotamian image fri the third or fourth millennium BC), no doubt singing of the despair and hopes of living peoples speaking , as amidst destruction and attack, they must still do, of their suffering and their longing for peace.

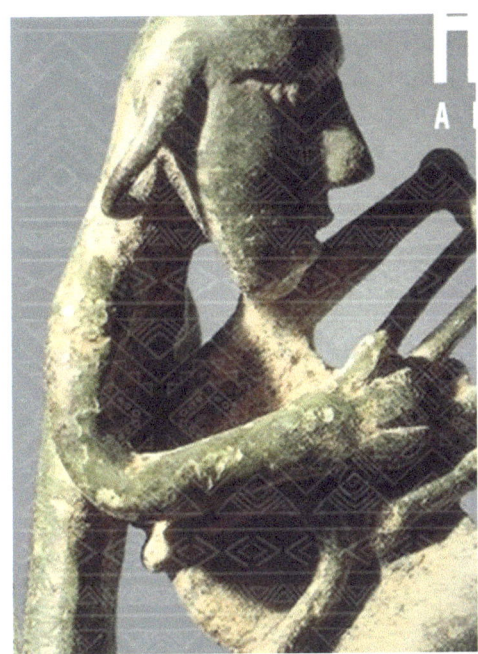

An earlier "Homer"

The pain of war [4]

Euripides

The Trojan women, by the fifth-century Greek tragedian Euripides, evokes the sorrows of war in sung verse by the Chorus—the voice of everyman, then, and now

His prize-winning play about the effect of sacking of Troy (Ilion) on the pitiful victims of war—its inevitable consequence ("collateral damage"as they call it now) —was produced in Athens in 415 BC in a time of war. It has remained popular ever since picking up the everlasting strain of compassion among humankind.

---

[4] *From Euripides The Trojan Women, translated Gilbert Murray.*

The sacrifice is gone and the sound of joy,
The dancing under the stars and the night-long prayer:
The Golden Images and the Moons of Troy,
The twelve Moons and the mighty names they bear:

My heart, my heart crieth, O Lord Zeus on high,
Were they all to thee as nothing, thou thronèd in the sky,
Thronèd in the fire-cloud, where a City, near to die,
Passeth in the wind and the flare?
Woe, woe, woe!

Thou of the Ages O wherefore fleëst thou?
Father that made us
 Tis we, thy children; shall no man aid us?
 Tis we, thy children! Seëst thou, seëst thou?
He seëth, only his heart is pitiless;
 And the land dies: yea, she,
She of the Mighty Cities perisheth citiless!
 Troy shall no more be!
Woe, woe, woe!

The lion shineth afar!
Fire in the deeps thereof,
Fire in the heights above,
 And crested walls of War!
As smoke on the wing of heaven
Climbeth and scattereth,
 Torn of the spear and driven,
 The land crieth for death:
O stormy battlements that red fire hath riven,
 And the sword's angry breath!

In praise of peace [5]
Aristophanes

"Peace" is the first of the remaining series of Greek peace plays by the comic dramatist Aristophanes. Produced in Athens in 422 BC during a lengthy war it won plaudits at the time and has been a favourite ever since, together with the rollicking and equally peace-seeking Lysistrata.

For all its comic and licentious language the play points perceptively to the attraction of war and to the poets who, as Erasmus brings out in the next extract, continually glorify it. But its central import is to laud the blessings of peace and remind us (so relevant still), of the seemingly innocuous but pernicious influence of armaments dealers and manufacturers. It was ever so.

As in other Greek plays the action, from which extracts are given below, proceeds through the intersection of prose conversation by everyday and usually comic characters and the sung poetic commentary by the Chorus.

CHORUS
Then came the shouting of victory from some and the groaning of defeat from others.

Oh, Muse! drive the War far from our city and come to preside over our dances, if you love me; come and celebrate the nuptials of the gods, the banquets of us mortals and the festivals of the fortunate; these are the themes that inspire thy most poetic songs. And should Carcinus come to beg thee for admission with his sons to thy chorus, refuse all traffic with them; remember they are but gelded birds, stork-necked dancers, mannikins about as tall as a pat of goat dung, in fact machine-made poets.

Such are the songs with which the Muse with the glorious hair inspires the able poet and which enchant the assembled populace, when the spring swallow twitters beneath the foliage …

SERVANT Take the knife and slaughter the sheep like a finished cook.
TRYGAEUS No, the goddess does not wish it
SERVANT And why not?
TRYGAEUS Blood cannot please Peace, so let us spill none upon her altar.
CHORUS I have no passion for battles;

---

[5] *From Aristophanes' comedy "Peace", translation by The Athenian Society, 1912.*

What I love, is to drink with good comrades in the corner by the fire when good dry wood, cut in the height of the summer, is crackling;

it is to cook pease on the coals and beechnuts among the embers, 'tis to kiss our pretty Thracian while my wife is at the bath.

Nothing is more pleasing, when the rain is sprouting our sowings, than to chat with some friend, saying, Tell me, what shall we do

The townsfolk are less ill-used, but that is how the husbandmen are treated by these men of war, the hated of the gods and of men, who know nothing but how to throw away their shield. For this reason, if it please heaven, I propose to call these rascals to account, for they are lions in times of peace, but sneaking foxes when it comes to fighting.
TRYGAEUS Thanks. Put them all down inside there, and come along quick to the banquet. Ah! Do you see that armourer yonder coming with a wry face?
A CREST-MAKER Alas! Alas! Trygaeus, you have ruined me utterly.
TRYGAEUS What! Won't the crests go any more, friend?
CREST-MAKER You have killed my business, my livelihood, and that of this poor lance-maker too.
TRYGAEUS Come, come, what are you asking for these two crests?
CREST-MAKER What do you bid for them?
TRYGAEUS What do I bid? Oh! I am ashamed to say. Still, as the clasp is of good workmanship, I would give two, even three measures of dried figs; I could use 'em for dusting the table.
CREST-MAKER All right, tell them to bring me the dried figs; 'tis always better than nothing.
TRYGAEUS Take them away, be off with your crests and get you gone; they are moulting, they are losing all their hair; I would not give a single fig for them.
A BREASTPLATE-MAKER Good gods, what am I going to do with this fine ten-minae breastplate, which is so splendidly made?
TRYGAEUS Oh, you will lose nothing over it.
BREASTPLATE-MAKER I will sell it to you at cost price.
HELMET-MAKER Cursed fate! I am ruined. Here are helmets, for which I gave a mina each. What I to do with them? Who will buy them?
TRYGAEUS Go and sell them to the Egyptians; they will do for measuring loosening medicines.(1)
A SPEAR-MAKER Ah! Poor helmet-maker, things are indeed in a bad way.
TRYGAEUS That man has no cause for complaint.
SPEAR-MAKER But helmets will be no more used.
TRYGAEUS Ah! Here come the guests, children from the table to relieve themselves; I fancy they also want to hum over what they will be singing presently. Hi! Child! What do you reckon to sing? Stand there and give me the opening line.

"Peace is the beauty of life"[6]
The great religions speak

These are mostly just short sayings: a multitude. They come from many authors, backgrounds and historical times, from antiquity onwards, all the more quoted and memorable for their brevity. They are the bedrock, consciously invoked or not, for what follows below (and, for all we know, long before too) in writing, in speech, and in song.

And in action too. In 1815 a Quaker was probably the first conscientious objector in the modern sense. Several Christian denominations have taken pacifist positions, notably the Quakers, (illustrated in a later section), Mennonites, Christadelphians, and Seventh Day Adventists. So too, independently, have many other brave individuals, moved by the consciousness of love for their fellow creature and protest against the defilement of God's beautiful universe.

The word "peace"' is not always there as such. But through the concepts of beauty, truth, love, friendship or forgiveness it is always somehow and somewhere present. For:

"Better than a thousand hollow words, is one word that brings peace".
Gautama Buddha

They will beat their swords into plowshares and their spears into pruning hooks. Nation will not take up sword against nation, nor will they train for war anymore.
The Old Testament, Book of Isaiah

Thus saith the LORD, Behold, I will extend peace to her like a river, and the glory of the Gentiles like a flowing stream
The Old Testament, Book of Isaiah

Seek peace and pursue it.
The Old Testament, Psalm 34

May God lift up his face onto you and give you peace.
The Old Testament, Book of Numbers

A generous heart, kind speech, and a life of service and compassion are the things which renew humanity.
Buddhist saying

---

[6] Sources: multiple hymn books anthologies, internet, and personal knowledge/memory.

Better than a thousand sayings is one word that brings peace.
Buddhist saying

Love your enemies, do good to those who hate you, bless those who curse you, pray for those who mistreat you.
The New Testament, Saint Matthew's Gospel

Blessed are the peace-makers for they are the children of God.
The New Testament, Saint Matthew's Gospel

Do not take revenge, my dear friends, but leave room for God's wrath, for it is written: "It is mine to avenge; I will repay," says the Lord. No. If your enemy is hungry, feed him. If he is thirsty, give him something to drink.
The New Testament, Letter of Paul to the Romans

We refrain from making war on our enemies. For Christ's soldiers possess nothing that they can lose more precious than their life, while their love goes out to their eternal life.
Justin Martyr, 2nd century AD

Whatever Christians would not wish others to do to them, they do not to others. And they comfort their oppressors and make them their friends; they do good to their enemies.
Aristides, *Apology,* 2nd century

It is better to suffer wrong than to inflict it, we should rather shed our own blood than stain our hands and our conscience with that of another.
Tertullian, *On Idolatry*, 3rd century

Murder, which in the case of an individual is admitted to be a crime, is called a virtue when it is committed wholesale.
Cyprian, Bishop of Carthage, 3rd century

And thus we may say of peace, as we have said of eternal life, that it is the end of our good; and the rather because the Psalmist says of the city of God… that final peace we are wishing to declare.
Augustine, *The City of God*, 5th century.

Make me a channel of your peace; it is in pardoning that we are pardoned.
St Francis of Assisi, 13th century

To our most bitter opponents we say: "We shall match your capacity to inflict suffering by our capacity to endure suffering. We shall meet your physical force with soul force. Do to us what you will, and we shall continue to love you".
Menno Simons, founder of the Mennonites,

Reply to False Accusations, 15th century

Some one dear to you can be loved with human love; but an enemy can only be loved with divine love.

Leo Tolstoy, *War and Peace*

That you need God more than anything, you know at all times in your heart. But don't you know also that God needs you—in the fullness of his eternity, *you*?

Martin Buber, *I and Thou*, 1923

I don't think of all the misery but of the beauty that still remains.

Anne Frank, *Diary* (died in Auschwitz concentration camp in 1945)

It took me a long time to understand that God is not the enemy of my enemies. God is not even the enemy of God's enemies.

Martin Niemoller, German theologian and Lutheran pastor (imprisoned in Germany during the 1939-45 World War)

Mother's love is peace. It need not be acquired, it need not be deserved.

Erich Fromm (1900-1980), German writer and psychiatrist

Peace cannot be kept by force; it can only be achieved by understanding.
Albert Einstein

Peace is the beauty of life. It is sunshine. It is the smile of a child, the love of a mother, the joy of a father, the togetherness of a family. It is the advancement of man, the victory of a just cause, the triumph of truth

Menachem Begin, Prime Minister of Israel, 1977

I refuse to accept the view that mankind is so tragically bound to the starless midnight of racism and war that the bright daybreak of peace and brotherhood can never become a reality ... Peace is not merely a distant goal that we seek, but a means by which we arrive at that goal.

Martin Luther King, 1964

In my own work for peace, I was very strongly inspired by my European experience. I always tell this story, and I do so because it is so simple yet so profound and so applicable to conflict resolution anywhere in the world. On my first visit to Strasbourg in 1979 as a member of the European Parliament. I went for a walk across the bridge from Strasbourg to Kehl. Strasbourg is in France. Kehl is in Germany. They are very close.

I stopped in the middle of the bridge and I meditated. There is Germany. There is France. If I had stood on this bridge 30 years ago after the end of the second world war when 25 million people lay dead across our continent for the second time in this century and if I had said: "Don't worry. In 30 years' time we will all be together in a new Europe, our

conflicts and wars will be ended and we will be working together in our common interests", I would have been sent to a psychiatrist.
   But it has happened
      John Hume, politician and political leader amidst the fraught conflicts of Northern Ireland, 1998

We can't *wait* for peace, we have to *work* for peace.
   The Parents Circle – Families Forum, a multi-ethnic, multi-religious group of people who lost family members in the struggle between Israel and Palestine

Only within the context of true peace can normal relations flourish between the people of the region .
   Crown Prince Abdullah of Saudi Arabia to the Arab League, 2002

"War is so twentieth century …"
"Have a heart"
"Make tea not war"
"Peace begins with peace"
"War just makes it worse"
                              Placards, anti-war march, London 2003

A tree begins with a seed.
                                                        Arabic proverb

Upendo kote amani (Swahili): Love everywhere, and peace.
                                                 Hip-hop singer, Kenya, 2008

Whenever people stretch out the hand of friendship towards me I am not going to refuse that hand.
   Martin McGuinness, political leader and peace negotiator, Northern Ireland.

The Town Mouse and the Country Mouse[7]
Aesop

Aesop's famous fables -- light tales with a moral, mostly expressed through the speech and actions of animal characters — were in ancient times attributed to Aesop, a slave and story-teller who lived in Greece in the seventh century BC. They were probably first written down in any extensive form in Latin, in verse, by Phaedrus, also a slave, during the first century AD but had been around in the oral tradition for several centuries before that.

This one gives us a very down-to-earth view of the blessings of peace in the sense of the absence of the conflicts and distractions that can be associated with stressful urban living.

A Town Mouse once upon a time went on a visit to his cousin in the country.

He was rough and ready, this cousin, but he loved his town friend and made him heartily welcome.

Beans and bacon, cheese and bread, were all he had to offer, but he offered them freely.

The Town Mouse rather turned up his long nose at this country fare, and said: "I cannot understand, Cousin, how you can put up with such poor food as this, but of course you cannot expect anything better in the country; come you with me and I will show you how to live. When you have been in town a week you will wonder how you could ever have stood a country life."

No sooner said than done: the two mice set off for the town and arrived at the Town Mouse's residence late at night.

"You will want some refreshment after our long journey" said the polite Town Mouse, and took his friend into the grand dining-room.

There they found the remains of a fine feast, and soon the two mice were eating up jellies and cakes and all that was nice.

Suddenly they heard growling and barking.

---

[7] Source: *Aesop's Fables*

"What is that?" said the Country Mouse.

"It is only the dogs of the house," answered the other.

"Only!" said the Country Mouse. "I do not like that music at my dinner."

Just at that moment the door flew open, in came two huge mastiffs, and the two mice had to scamper down and run off.

"Good-bye, Cousin," said the Country Mouse, "What! going so soon?" said the other.

"Yes," he replied; "Better beans and bacon in peace than cakes and ale in fear".

War and Peace in the Qur'an [8]
The Prophet Mohammad

For Islam peace is the norm, war an exception. The word "Islam" itself is an Arabic word which has two meanings: submission to the will of God and "peace". A Muslim is thus defined as "someone who attains peace by submitting to the will of God". One of the 99 names of God in the Qur'an *is* Al-Salam *(The Source of Peace).*

Thus does not mean, however, that Islam is a pacifist religion. War is a necessary evil in situations where this seems to be the only way to defeat or stop greater evil after all other efforts have failed. As detailed below however it must only be conducted under certain quite stringent restrictions — an important set of principles now widely recognised in the legal concept of a "just war" by international thinkers and practitioners.

The commonly used word jihad *is often misunderstood as implying aggression and forcible conversion to Islam. On the contrary it essentially means "to strive" or "to struggle" in the way that the* Qur'an *expects believers to strive in submitting to the will of God in their everyday lives.*

There are different levels of jihad. *"The Greater Jihad" is the personal spiritual struggle or effort of every Muslim to follow the teachings of God in their own lives by, for example, overcoming things such as anger, greed, pride and hatred; forgiving someone who has hurt them; working for social justice. '"The Lesser* Jihad'"*is the struggle to build a good and just society free from oppression and to use proportionate force if necessary to repel an evil.*

Thus, jihad *is used in a general sense. If* war *is meant, the word* qital *(fighting) is used. The term "Holy War" is alien to Islam and this term is never used in the* Qur'an *or in any of the sayings of the Prophet.*

Contrary to widespread historical misconception jihad *was never used to spread Islam. That is why, for example, we find that despite ruling for eight centuries in the West in Spain and in the East in India, the majority of the population remained Christians and Hindus respectively.*

Owing perhaps to the background of the seventh century Qur'an and (somewhat later) Hadith, both coming from a rich oral tradition, reflections on peace again appear scattered throughout the foundational texts that we have inherited today, but their overall import is clear.

God invites all to the Abode of Peace and He guides whom He wills to the

---

[8] Source: the *quran* (*Koran*).

Straight Path.

Reconciliation is better even though people's souls are swayed by greed. If you act righteously and be pious, God is Well Aware of what you do.

And if two factions among the believers should fight, then make reconciliation between the two. But if one of them oppresses the other, then fight against the one that oppresses until it returns to the ordinance of God. And if it returns, then make reconciliation between them in justice and act equitably. Indeed, God loves those who act equitably.

If the enemy is inclined towards peace, you should also incline towards peace, and trust in God; for He is the One that hears and knows all things. And if they should deceive you, then remember that God is Sufficient for you as He supports you with His help and with the believers.

Fight in the way of God against those who fight against you, but do not transgress. Indeed God does not love the transgressors.

Permission to fight is given to those against whom war is made, because they have been wronged-and Allah indeed has power to help them— Those who have been driven out from their homes unjustly only because they said, Our Lord is God-And if God did not repel some people by means of others, there would surely have been pulled down cloisters and churches and synagogues and mosques, wherein the name of Allah is oft mentioned. And God will surely help the one who helps Him. Indeed God is the Powerful, the Almighty.

A war, when necessary as a last resort, has to follow strict rules in order to be legitimate:

• The opponent must have started the fighting
• It must not be fought to gain territory
• It must be launched by the Caliph or recognised leader
• It must be fought to bring about good – something that God would approve of
• It must be a last resort – all other ways of solving the problem must have been tried
• Innocent people should not be killed; women, children or old people should not be killed or hurt
• Women must not be raped or abused in any way
• Enemies must be treated with justice
• Wounded enemy soldiers must be treated in exactly the same way as one's own soldiers
• The war must stop as soon as the enemy asks for peace
• Property must not be damaged
• Poisoning of wells is forbidden (chemical or biological warfare might be

a modern analogy, or the cutting off of access to water).

Some of the other well-known rules pertaining to war, based on the direct teachings of the Prophet (Hadith), are as follows:

- Muslims are forbidden altogether to mutilate the dead.
- Muslims are forbidden to resort to cheating.
- Children, women, the old and other non-combatants are not to be killed.
- Priests and religious functionaries and religious leaders are not to be interfered with at all.
- When Muslims enter enemy territory, they should not strike terror into the general population. They should permit no ill-treatment of common people.
- A Muslim army should not camp in a place where it causes inconvenience to the general public. When it marches it should take care not to block the road nor cause discomfort to other wayfarers.
- No disfigurement of face is to be permitted.
- The least possible losses should be inflicted upon the enemy.
- When prisoners of war are put under guard, those closely related should be placed together.
- Prisoners should live in comfort. Muslims should care more for the comfort of their prisoners than for their own.
- Emissaries and delegates from other countries should be held in great respect. Any mistakes or discourtesies they commit should be ignored.
- If a Muslim commits the sin of ill-treating a prisoner of war, atonement is to be made by releasing the prisoner without ransom.
- When a Muslim takes charge of a prisoner of war, the latter is to be fed and clothed in the same way as the Muslim himself.
- Public buildings and fruit-bearing trees (and food crops) are not to be damaged.

The Holy Prophet (in the *Hadith*) was so insistent on these rules for a fighting army that he declared that whoever did not observe these rules, would not be fighting for God but for his own mean self.

Dulce bellum inexpertis [9]
("War is great when you're not the one suffering it/ on the front line", or (modern translation), "War's okay if you're in the White House")
Erasmus Desiderius of Rotterdam

The commentary on the proverb dulce bellum inexpertis *from which extracts are given below comes from the treatment of peace in the huge* Adagia *collection (proverbs with commentaries) first published in Paris in 1500 AD, and then in increasingly lengthy instalments in Europe over the early years of the sixteenth century gathered by the noted humanist scholar Desiderius Erasmus of Rotterdam. It was written in a era of warfare - Erasmus knew only too well what he was talking about.*

It is one of the great works of the Renaissance, on the cusp of the movement from script to print, a best-seller in both modes – and still.

Though often taken as the founding tract of pacifism Erasmus' treatment is somewhat broader in scope. Nevertheless, or perhaps because of this wider vision, it remains one of the most profoundly and passionately argued considerations of the moral and practical benefits of peace and the disasters of war.

Pragmatic as well as principled this treatment is still of significance today.

It is both an elegant proverb, and among all others, by the writings of many excellent authors, full often and solemnly used, *Dulce bellum inexpertis*, that is to say, War is sweet to them that know it not.

There be some things among mortal men's businesses, in the which how great danger and hurt there is, a man cannot perceive till he make a proof. The love and friendship of a great man is sweet to them that be not expert: he that hath had thereof experience, is afraid.

It seemeth to be a gay and a glorious thing, to strut up and down among the nobles of the court, and to be occupied in the king's business; but old men, to whom that thing by long experience is well known, do gladly abstain themselves from such felicity. It seemeth a pleasant thing to be in love with a young ; but that is unto them that have not yet perceived how much grief and bitterness is in such love. So after this manner of fashion, this proverb may be applied to every business that is adjoined with great peril and with many evils: the which no man will take on hand, but he that is young and wanteth experience of things.

---

[9] *Well-known ancient proverb, used by Erasmus as the basis of his long essay on peace.*

Aristotle, in his book of Rhetoric, showeth the cause why youth is more bold, and contrariwise old age more fearful: for unto young men lack of experience is cause of great boldness, and to the other, experience of many griefs engendereth fear and doubting.

Then if there be anything in the world that should be taken in hand with fear and doubting, yea, that ought by all manner of means to be fled, to be withstood with prayer, and to be clean avoided, verily it is war; than which nothing is either more wicked, or more wretched, or that more farther destroyeth, or that never hand cleaveth sorer to, or doth more hurt, or is more horrible, and briefly to speak, nothing doth worse become a man (I will not say a Christian man) than war. And yet it is a wonder to speak of, how nowadays in every place, how lightly, and how for every trifling matter, it is taken in hand, how outrageously and barbarously it is gested and done, not only of heathen people, but also of Christian men; not only of secular men, but also of priests and bishops; not only of young men and of them that have no experience, but also of old men and of those that so often have had experience; not only of the common and movable vulgar people, but most specially of the princes, whose duty had been, by wisdom and reason, to set in a good order and to pacify the light and hasty movings of the foolish multitude.

Neither do there lack lawyers, nor yet divines, the which are ready with their firebrands to kindle these things so abominable, and they encourage them that else were cold, and they privily provoke those to it that were weary thereof. And by these means it is come to that pass that war is a thing now so well accepted, that men wonder at him that is not pleased therewith. It is so much approved, that it is counted a wicked thing (and I had almost said heresy) to reprove this one thing, the which as it is above all other things most mischievous, so it is most wretched.

But how more justly should this be wondered at, what evil spirit, what pestilence, what mischief, and what madness put first in man's mind a thing so beyond measure beastly, that this most pleasant and reasonable creature Man, the which Nature hath brought forth to peace and benevolence, which one alone she hath brought forth to the help and succour of all other, should with so wild wilfulness, with so mad rages, run headlong one to destroy another? At the which thing he shall also much more marvel, whosoever would withdraw his mind from the opinions of the common people, and will turn it to behold the very pure strength and nature of things; and will apart behold with philosophical eyes the image of man on the one side, and the picture of war on the other side.

Then first of all if one would consider well but the behaviour and shape of man's body shall he not forthwith perceive that Nature, or rather God, hath shaped this creature, not to war, but to friendship, not to destruction, but to health, not to wrong, but to kindness and benevolence? For whereas

Nature hath armed all other beasts with their own armour, as the violence of the bulls she hath armed with horns, the ramping lion with claws; to the boar she hath given the gnashing tusks; she hath armed the elephant with a long trump snout, besides his great huge body and hardness of the skin; she hath fenced the crocodile with a skin as hard as a plate; to the dolphin fish she hath given fins instead of a dart; the porcupine she defendeth with thorns; the ray and thornback with sharp prickles; to the cock she hath given strong spurs; some she fenceth with a shell, some with a hard hide, as it were thick leather, or bark of a tree; some she provideth to save by swiftness of flight, as doves; and to some she hath given venom instead of a weapon; to some she hath given a much horrible and ugly look, she hath given terrible eyes and grunting voice; and she hath also set among some of them continual dissension and debate—man alone she hath brought forth all naked, weak, tender, and without any armour, with most soft flesh and smooth skin.

There is nothing at all in all his members that may seem to be ordained to war, or to any violence. I will not say at this time, that where all other beasts, anon as they are brought forth, they are able of themselves to get their food. Man alone cometh so forth, that a long season after he is born, he dependeth altogether on the help of others. He can neither speak nor go, nor yet take meat; he desireth help only by his infant crying: so that a man may, at the least way, by this conject, that this creature alone was born all to love and amity, which specially increaseth and is fast knit together by good turns done eftsoons of one to another. And for this cause Nature would, that a man should not so much thank her, for the gift of life, which she hath given unto him, as he should thank kindness and benevolence, whereby he might evidently understand himself, that he was altogether dedicate and bounden to the gods of graces, that is to say, to kindness, benevolence, and amity.

And besides this Nature hath given unto man a countenance not terrible and loathly, as unto other brute beasts; but meek and demure, representing the very tokens of love and benevolence. She hath given him amiable eyes, and in them assured marks of the inward mind. She hath ordained him arms to clip and embrace. She hath given him the wit and understanding to kiss: whereby the very minds and hearts of men should be coupled together, even as though they touched each other. Unto man alone she hath given laughing, a token of good cheer and gladness. To man alone she hath given weeping tears, as it were a pledge or token of meekness and mercy. Yea, and she hath given him a voice not threatening and horrible, as unto other brute beasts, but amiable and pleasant. Nature not yet content with all this, she hath given unto man alone the commodity of speech and reasoning: the which things verily may specially both get and nourish benevolence, so that nothing at all should be done among men by violence…

There hath been hitherto enough spilt of Christian man's blood. We have showed pleasure enough to the enemies of the Christian religion. And if the common people, as they are wont, make any disturbance, let the princes bridle and quail them, which princes ought to be the selfsame thing in the commonweal that the eye is in the body, and the reason in the soul. Again, if the princes make any trouble, it is the part of good prelates by their wisdom and gravity to pacify and assuage such commotion. Or else, at the least, we being satiate with continual wars, let the desire of peace a little move us …

They that had liefer hear of proverbs, than either of peace or of war, will think that I have tarried longer about this digression than is meet for the declaration of a proverb.

Hymns, songs and blessings[10]
Yearners for peace through the centuries

Peace has been constantly sought through the ages: expressed, in personal terms; in beautiful words and tunes; sung too in tigetherness, and as a source of consolation.

Below are a small selection of the many hymns and blessings inspired by the deep longing for peace. They have been sung and composed by poets and yearners for peace from many backgrounds, educated and not, in many lands and languages, and across the ages.

Shalom, my friends,
Shalom, my friends,
Shalom, shalom.
Till we meet again,
Till we meet again,
Shalom, shalom.

Hebrew folk song (translator unknown).

Often sung as a round, this uses the lovely Hebrew word "shalom", that, richer than the English "peace", indicates not just the absence of conflict but completeness, harmony, wholeness, not least the harmony of the universe.

Fearlessness, singleness of soul, the will
Always to strive for wisdom; opened hand
And governed appetites; and piety,
And love of lonely study; humbleness,
Uprightness, heed to injure nought which lives
Truthfulness, slowness unto wrath, a mind
That lightly letteth go what others prize;
 And equanimity, and charity
 Which spieth no man's faults; and tenderness
Towards all that suffer

Bhagavad Gita

The peace of the earth be with you,
The peace of the heavens too;
The peace of the rivers be with you,
The peace of the oceans too.
Deep peace falling over you;
God's peace growing in you.

Guatemalan song (unknown translator)

---

[10] Sources: taken, variously, from many hymnbooks, anthologies and the internet; also from personal knowledge and memory.

I'm gonna lay down ma heavy load,
down by the riverside,
down by the riverside,
down by the riverside

I'm gonna lay down ma heavy load,
 down by the riverside
and I ain't a gonna study war no more.

Chorus (repeated ad lib)
I ain't gonna study war no more,
I ain't gonna study war no more,
I ain't gonna study war no more

I'm gonna lay down my sword and shield,
down by the riverside
down by the riverside,
down by the riverside

I'm gonna lay down my sword and shield,
down by the riverside
and I ain't gonna study war no more.
Chorus
I'm gonna put on ma traveling shoes,
down by the riverside
down by the riverside,
down by the riverside
I ain't gonna study war no more …
Chorus
I'm gonna put on ma long white robe
down by the riverside
down by the riverside,
down by the riverside …
Chorus
I'm gonna put on my starry crown,
down by the riverside
down by the riverside,
down by the riverside

and I ain't gonna study war no more …

Negro spiritual (verbally transmitted, original author unknown). It alludes to the *Old Testament* "nation shall not lift up sword against nation, neither shall they learn war any more". Further verses are also sometimes sung, with constant repetition, as (typical of oral tradition) inspired on the occasion.

Break forth, O beauteous heavenly light,
and usher in the morning.
You shepherds, shudder not with fright,
but hear the angel's warning.
This child, now weak in infancy,
our confidence and joy shall be,
the power of Satan breaking,
our peace eternal making.
          Chorale from Bach's *St Matthew Passion* (translated from the German by John Troutbeck)

It came upon a midnight clear,
That glorious song of old,
From angels bending near the earth,
To touch their harps of gold:
"Peace on the earth, goodwill to men,
From heaven's all-gracious King."
The world in solemn stillness lay,
To hear the angels sing.

Still through the cloven skies they come,
With peaceful wings unfurled,
And still their heavenly music floats
O'er all the weary world;
Above its sad and lowly plains,
They bend on hovering wing,
And ever o'er its babel sounds
The blessèd angels sing.

Yet with the woes of sin and strife
The world has suffered long;
Beneath the angel-strain have rolled
Two thousand years of wrong;
And man, at war with man, hears not
The love-song which they bring;
O hush the noise, ye men of strife,
And hear the angels sing.

For lo! the days are hastening on,
By prophet bards foretold,
When with the ever-circling years
Comes round the age of gold
When peace shall over all the earth
Its ancient splendors fling,
And the whole world give back the song
Which now the angels sing.

Carol, Edmund Sears

Sweet Peace, where dost thou dwell?
I humbly crave,
Let me once know.
I sought thee in a secret cave,
And ask'd, if Peace were there,
A hollow wind did seem to answer, No:
Go seek elsewhere.

I did; and going did a rainbow note:
Surely, thought I,
This is the lace of Peace's coat:
I will search out the matter.
But while I looked the clouds immediately
Did break and scatter.

Then went I to a garden and did spy
A gallant flower,
The crown-imperial: Sure, said I,
Peace at the root must dwell.
But when I digged, I saw a worm devour
What showed so well.

At length I met a rev'rend good old man;
Whom when for Peace

I did demand, he thus began:
There was a Prince of old
At Salem dwelt, who lived with good increase
Of flock and fold.

He sweetly lived; yet sweetness did not save
His life from foes.
But after death out of his grave
There sprang twelve stalks of wheat;
Which many wond'ring at, got some of those
To plant and set.

It prospered strangely, and did soon disperse
Through all the earth:
For they that taste it do rehearse
That virtue lies therein;
A secret virtue, bringing peace and mirth
By flight of sin.

Take of this grain, which in my garden grows,

And grows for you;
Make bread of it: and that repose
And peace, which ev'ry where
With so much earnestness you do pursue,
Is only there.

George Herbert

When will you ever, Peace, wild wood-dove, shy wings shut,
Your round me roaming end, and under be my boughs?
When, when, Peace, will you, Peace? I'll not play hypocrite
To own my heart: I yield you do come sometimes; but
That piecemeal peace is poor peace. What pure peace allows
Alarms of wars, the daunting wars, the death of it?

O surely, reaving Peace, my Lord should leave in lieu
Some good! And so he does leave Patience exquisite,
That plumes to Peace thereafter. And when Peace here does house
He comes with work to do, he does not come to coo,
He comes to brood and sit.

Gerard Manley Hopkins

My Soul, there is a country
Afar beyond the stars,
Where stands a winged sentry
All skillful in the wars;
There, above noise and danger
Sweet Peace sits, crown'd with smiles,
And One born in a manger
Commands the beauteous files.

He is thy gracious friend
Ahd (O my Soul awake!)
Did in pure love descend,
To die here for thy sake.
If thou canst get but thither,
There grows the flow'r of peace,
The rose that cannot wither,
Thy fortress, and thy ease.

Leave then thy foolish ranges,
For none can thee secure,
But One, who never changes,
Thy God, thy life, thy cure.

Henry Vaughan

Peace without Justice is a low estate,

43

A coward cringing to an iron Fate!
But Peace through Justice is the great ideal,
We'll pay the price of war to make it real.

        Henry Van Dyke

Jehovah-Shalom. The Lord Send Peace
Jesus! whose blood so freely stream'd
To satisfy the law's demand;
By Thee from guilt and wrath redeem'd,
Before the Father's face I stand.

To reconcile offending man,
Make Justice drop her angry rod;
What creature could have form'd the plan,
Or who fulfil it but a God?

No drop remains of all the curse,
For wretches who deserved the whole;
No arrows dipt in wrath to pierce
The guilty, but returning soul.

Peace by such means so dearly bought,
What rebel could have hoped to see?
Peace by his injured Sovereign wrought,
His Sovereign fasten'd to a tree.

Now, Lord, Thy feeble worm prepare!
For strife with earth and hell begins;
Conform and gird me for the war;
They hate the soul that hates his sins.

Let them in horrid league agree!
They may assault, they may distress;
But cannot quench Thy love to me,
Nor rob me of the Lord my peace.
  William Cowper (referring to *Old Testament, Book of* Judges, vi.25)

Those ends in war the best contentment bring,
Whose peace is made up with a pardoning.

        Robert Herrick

Dear Lord and Father of mankind,
Forgive our foolish ways;
Reclothe us in our rightful mind,
In purer lives Thy service find,
In deeper reverence, praise.

Drop Thy still dews of quietness,
Till all our strivings cease;
Take from our souls the strain and stress,
And let our ordered lives confess
The beauty of Thy peace.

Breathe through the heats of our desire
Thy coolness and Thy balm;
Let sense be dumb, let flesh retire;
Speak through the earthquake, wind, and fire,
O still, small voice of calm.

John Greenleaf Whittier

Deep peace of the running wave to you.
Deep peace of the flowing air to you.
Deep peace o the quiet earth to you.
Deep peace of the shining stars to you.
Deep peace of the gentle night to you.
Moon and stars pour their healing light on you.
Deep peace of Christ,
of Christ the light of the world to you.
Deep peace of Christ to you.
    (ancient Gaelic blessing, now often sung to John Rutter's beautiful modern setting)

The Lord bless you and keep you
The Lord make his face to shine upon you
and be gracious unto you.

The Lord lift up his countenance upon you
and give you peace.

Amen.
    (sung version of verses from *The Old Testament, Book of Numbers*)

An Exhortation to Peace and Unity[11]
John Bunyan

The authorship of this work has been called in question but it is given here for its influence both at the time and later. Published in 1688, it originated, the author states, in a sermon on a text from Paul's Letter to the Ephesians *on "the unity of the Spirit in the bond of peace". It is in keeping with the general spirit of this inspired preacher's work, author among other things of the (dreamed) classic,* The Pilgrim's Progress.

Bunyan suffered for his views and nonconformist activities (principally his preaching), as after the ending of religious tolerance with the restoration of the monarchy in 1660, he was indicted and imprisoned for 12 years in Bedford County Jail, a building, which, like many churches, long survived the ravages of time, as, too, has his striking likeness in the centre of Bedford.

Beloved, religion is the great bond of human society; and it were well if itself were kept within the bond of unity; and that it may so be, let us, according to the text, use our utmost endeavours "to keep the unity of the Spirit in the bond of peace."

These words contain a counsel and a caution: the counsel is, That we endeavour to keep the unity of the Spirit; the caution is, That we do it in the bond of peace; as if I should say, I would have you live in unity, but yet I would have you to be careful that you do not purchase unity with the breach of charity.

Let us therefore be cautious that we do not so press after unity in practice and opinion as to break the bond of peace and affection.
In the handling of these words, I shall observe this method.
I. I shall open the sense of the text.
II. I shall shew wherein this unity and peace consist.
III. I shall shew you the fruits and benefits of it, together with nine inconveniences and mischiefs that attend those churches where unity and peace is wanting.

---

[11] Source: from http://www.gutenberg.org/ebooks/3614/.

IV. And, lastly, I shall give you twelve directions and motives for the obtaining of it …

II.
1. That believing that the Son of God died for the sins of men is necessary to salvation, I prove by these texts, which tell us, that he that doth not believe shall be damned, Mark xvi. 16; John iii. 36; Rom. x. 9.

That it is also necessary to church-communion appears from Matt. xvi. 16–18. Peter having confessed that Christ was the Son of the living God, Christ thereupon assures Peter, that upon this rock, viz., this profession of faith, or this Christ which Peter had confessed, he would build his church, and the gates of hell should not prevail against it. And, 1 Cor. iii. 11, the apostle having told the Corinthians that they were God's building, presently adds, that they could not be built upon any foundation but upon that which was laid, which was Jesus Christ. All which proves, that Christian society is founded upon the profession of Christ; and not only scripture, but the laws of right reason, dictate this, that some rules and orders must be observed for the founding all society, which must be consented to by all that will be of it. Hence it comes to pass, that to own Christ as the Lord and head of Christians is essential to the founding of Christian society.

2. The Scriptures have declared, that this faith gives the professors of it a right to baptism, as in the case of the eunuch, Acts viii …

.
3. Holiness of life is essential to church-communion, because it seems to be the reason why Christ founded a church in the world, viz., that men might thereby be watched over, and kept from falling; and that if any be overtaken with a fault, he that is spiritual might restore him, that by this means men and women might be preserved without blame to the coming of Christ; and the grace of God teacheth us to deny ungodliness and worldly lusts, and to live soberly and uprightly in this present evil world3. Unity and peace consists in all as with one shoulder practising and putting in execution the things we do know; Phil. iii. 16. "Nevertheless, whereto we have already attained, let us walk by the same rule, and mind the same thing." How sad is it to see our zeal consume us and our precious time in things doubtful and disputable, while we are not concerned nor affected with the practice of those indisputable things we all agree in! We all know charity to be the great command, and yet how few agree to practise it? We all know they that labour in the word and doctrine are worthy of double honour; and that God hath ordained, that they which preach the gospel should live of the gospel. These duties, however others have cavilled at them, I know you agree in them, and are persuaded of your duty therein: but where is your zeal to practise? O how well would it be with churches, if they were but half as zealous for the

great, and plain, and indisputable things, and the more chargeable and costly things of religion, as they are for things doubtful or less necessary, or for things that are no charge to them, and cost them nothing but the breath of contention, though that may be too great a price for the small things they purchase with it!

But further, Do we not all agree, that men that preach the gospel should do it like workmen that need not be ashamed? and yet how little is this considered by many preachers, who never consider before they speak of what they say, or whereof they affirm! How few give themselves to study that they may be approved! How few meditate and give themselves to these things, that their profiting may appear to all!

For the Lord's sake let us unite to practise those things we know; and if we would have more talents, let us all agree to improve those we have.

See the spirit that was among the primitive professors, that knowing and believing how much it concerned them in the propagating of Christianity, to shew forth love to one another (that so all might know them to be Christ's disciples), rather than there should be any complainings among them, they sold all they had. O how zealous were these to practise, and as with one shoulder to do that that was upon their hearts for God! I might further add, how often have we agreed in our judgment? and hath it not been upon our hearts, that this and the other thing is good to be done, to enlighten the dark world, and to repair the breaches of churches, and to raise up those churches that now lie gasping, and among whom the soul of religion is expiring? But what do we more than talk of them? Do not most decline these things, when they either call for their purses or their persons to help in this and such like works as these? Let us then, in what we know, unite, that we may put it in practice, remembering, that if we know these things, we shall be happy if we do them.

4. This unity and peace consists in our joining and agreeing to pray for, and to press after, those truths we do not know. The disciples in the primitive times were conscious of their imperfections, and therefore they with one accord continued in prayer and supplications. If we were more in the sense of our ignorance and imperfections, we should carry it better towards those that differ from us: then we should abound more in the spirit of meekness and forbearance, that thereby we might bring others (or be brought by others) to the knowledge of the truth: this would make us go to God, and say with Elihu, Job xxxiv. 32, "That which we know not, teach thou us." Brethren, did we but all agree that we were erring in many things, we should soon agree to go to God, and pray for more wisdom and revelation of his mind and will concerning us.

But here is our misery, that we no sooner receive any thing for truth, but we presently ascend the chair of infallibility with it, as though in this we could not err: hence it is we are impatient of contradiction, and become uncharitable to those that are not of the same mind; but now a consciousness that we may mistake, or that if my brother err in one thing, I may err in another; this will unite us in affection, and engage us to press after perfection, according to that of the apostle; Phil. iii. 13–15, "Brethren, I count not myself to have apprehended: But this one thing I do, forgetting those things which are behind, and reaching forth unto those things which are before, I press toward the mark, for the prize of the high calling of God in Christ Jesus. And if in any thing ye be otherwise minded, God shall reveal even this unto you."

O then that we could but unite and agree to go to God for one another, in confidence that he will teach us; and that if any one of us want wisdom (as who of us does not), we might agree to ask of God, who giveth to all men liberally, and upbraideth no man! Let us, like those people spoken of in the 2d of Isaiah, say to one another, "Come, let us go to the Lord, for he will teach us of his ways, and we will walk in his paths."

5. This unity and peace mainly consists in unity of love and affection: this is the great and indispensable duty of all Christians; by this they are declared Christ's disciples; And hence it is that love is called "the great commandment," "the old commandment," and "the new commandment;" that which was commanded in the beginning, and will remain to the end, yea, and after the end. 1 Cor. xiii. 8, "Charity never faileth; but whether there be tongues, they shall cease; or whether there be knowledge, it shall vanish away." And ver. 13, "And now abideth faith, hope, charity; but the greatest of these is charity." And Col. iii. 14, "Above all these things, put on charity, which is the bond of perfectness;" because charity is the end of the commandment, 1 Tim. i. 5. Charity is therefore called "the royal law;" as though it had a superintendency over other laws, and doubtless is a law to which other laws must give place, when they come in competition with it; "above all things, therefore, have fervent charity among yourselves; for charity shall cover the multitude of sins;" 1 Pet. iv. 8. Let us therefore live in unity and peace, and the God of love and peace will be with us.
That you may so do, let me remind you (in the words of a learned man), that the unity of the church is a unity of love and affection, and not a bare uniformity of practice and opinion.

III
Having shewn you wherein this unity consists, I now come to the third general thing propounded: and that is, to shew you the fruits and benefits of unity and peace, together with the mischiefs and inconveniences that attend those churches where unity and peace are wanting.

1. Unity and peace is a duty well-pleasing to God, who is styled the author of peace and not of confusion. In all the churches God's Spirit

rejoiceth in the unity of our spirits; but on the other hand, where strife and divisions are, there the Spirit of God is grieved. Hence it is that the apostle no sooner calls upon the Ephesians not to grieve the Spirit of God, but he presently subjoins us a remedy against that evil, that they put away bitterness and evil-speaking, and be kind one to another, and tender-hearted, forgiving one another, even as God for Christ's sake hath forgiven them; Eph. iv. 30, 32.

2. As unity and peace is pleasing to God, and rejoiceth his Spirit, so it rejoiceth the hearts and spirits of God's people. Unity and peace brings heaven down upon earth among us: hence it is that the apostle tells us, Rom. iv. 17, that "the kingdom of God is not meat and drink, but righteousness and peace and joy in the Holy Ghost." Where unity and peace is, there is heaven upon earth; by this we taste the first fruits of that blessed estate we shall one day live in the fruition of; when we shall come "to the general assembly and church of the first-born, whose names are written in heaven, and to God the judge of all, and to the spirits of just men made perfect;" Heb. xii. 23.

This outward peace of the church (as a learned man observes) distils into peace of conscience, and turns writings and readings of controversy into treatises of mortification and devotion.

And the Psalmist tells us, that it is not only good, but pleasant for brethren to dwell together in unity, Psalm cxxxiii. But where unity and peace is wanting, there are storms and troubles; "where envy and strife is, there is confusion and every evil work;" James iii. 16. It is the outward peace of the church that increaseth our inward joy; and the peace of God's house gives us occasion to eat our meat with gladness in our own houses, Acts ii. 46.

3. The unity and peace of the church makes communion of saints desirable. What is it that embitters church-communion, and makes it burdensome, but divisions? Have you not heard many complain, that they are weary of church-communion, because of church-contention? but now where unity and peace is, there Christians long for communion ...

III

Where unity and peace is wanting, there is evil surmising and evil speaking, to the damage and disgrace, if not to the ruining, of one another; Gal. v. 14, 15. The whole law is fulfilled in one word, "Thou shalt love thy neighbour as thyself. But if you bite and devour one another, take heed you be not consumed one of another." No sooner the bond of charity is broken, which is as a wall about Christians, but soon they begin to make havock and spoil of one another; then there is raising evil reports, and taking up evil reports, against each other. Hence it is that whispering and backbiting proceeds, and going from house to house to blazon the faults and infirmities of others: hence it is that we watch for the haltings of one another, and do inwardly rejoice at the miscarriages of others, saying in our hearts, "ha! ha! so we would have it:" but now where unity and peace is, there is charity; and where charity is, there we are willing to hide the faults, and cover the nakedness, of our brethren. "Charity thinketh no evil;" 1 Cor. xiii. 5; and therefore it cannot surmise, neither will it speak evil.

Where unity and peace is wanting, there can be no great matters enterprised … Peace is to churches as walls to a city; nay, unity hath defended cities that had no walls.

Quaker witnesses over the centuries: Peace affirming and its dilemmas[12]

Quaker voices

Ask anyone about the essential beliefs of the Society of Friends and you will hear something about "Friends' historic peace testimony'". "Quakers don't fight in wars" is something specific that people remember above all about this set of beliefs.

In a world where it is considered acceptable, indeed praiseworthy, to go to war and kill other people, in a world where we have learned to define success, amass our fortunes or win arguments at the expense of others like us (our enemies) who lose out, the perception that 'Quakers are peacemakers' sets Friends apart and makes them visible. Their Peace Testimony is without question the best known and best loved of the Quaker testimonies.

Its roots lie in the personal experience of the love and power of Christ which marked the founders of the Quaker movement. It is dominated by a vision of the world transformed by Christ who lives in the hearts of all. Friends seek to make the vision real by putting emphasis on Christian practice rather than primarily on any particular dogma or ideological system.

It is a practical religion. They recognise the realities of evil and conflict, but hold that it is contrary to the spirit of Christ to use war and violence as means to deal with them.

The Peace Testimony has been a source of inspiration to Friends through the centuries, for it points to a way of life which embraces all human relationships. These pacifist convictions represent a strongly held and inspiring position among Friends but in the closing years of the twentieth century they faced a bewildering array of social and international challenges, which have widened the relevance of the Peace Testimony from the issue of peace and war between states to the problems of tensions and conflicts in all their forms. Thus we are brought closer to the witness of early Friends -   of more recent ones too (as in the moving https://www.gofundme.com/f/everest-mountain-climb-a-matter-of-

---

[12] *Sources: from* http://www.quaker.org/minnfm/peace/index.htm/ *and Quaker Faith and Practice chapter 24 .*

principle/); they did not draw a hard and fast distinction between the various Quaker testimonies, but saw them as a seamless expression of the universal spirit of Christ that dwells in the hearts of all.

I told [the Commonwealth Commissioners] I lived in the virtue of that life and power that took away the occasion of all wars… I told them I was come into the covenant of peace which was before wars and strife were.

George Fox, 1651

A good end cannot sanctify evil means; nor must we ever do evil, that good may come of it… It is as great presumption to send our passions upon God's errands, as it is to palliate them with God's name … We are too ready to retaliate, rather than forgive, or gain by love and information. And yet we could hurt no man that we believe loves us. Let us then try what Love will do: for if men did once see we love them, we should soon find they would not harm us. Force may subdue, but Love gains: and he that forgives first, wins the laurel.

William Penn, 1693

Most, if not all, people admit the transcendent excellency of peace. All who adopt the petition, 'Thy kingdom come', pray for its universal establishment. Some people then must begin to fulfil the evangelical promise, and cease to learn war any more. Now, friends, seeing these things cannot be controverted, how do we long that your whole conversation be as becometh the Gospel; and that while any of us are professing to scruple war, they may not in some parts of their conduct be inconsistent with that profession! … Friends, it is an awful thing to stand forth to the nation as the advocates of inviolable peace; and our testimony loses its efficacy in proportion to the want of consistency in any… And we can serve our country in no way more availingly, nor more acceptably to him who holds its prosperity at his disposal, than by contributing, all that in us lies, to increase the number of meek, humble, and self-denying Christians.

Guard against placing your dependence on fleets and armies; be peaceable yourselves, in words and actions, and pray to the Father of the Universe that he would breathe the spirit of reconciliation into the hearts of his erring and contending creatures.end.

London Yearly Meeting, 1804/5, during the Napoleonic Wars

We believe that the Spirit of Christ will ultimately redeem national as well as individual life. We believe further that, as all church history shows, the human means will be the faithful witness borne by Christ's disciples. It has been well said: 'It seems to be the will of Him, who is infinite in wisdom, that light upon great subjects should first arise and be gradually spread through the faithfulness of individuals in acting up to their own convictions.' This was the secret of the power of the early Church. The blood of the Christians proved a fruitful seed. In like manner the staunchness of early Friends and others to their conscientious convictions in the seventeenth century won the battle of religious freedom for England. We covet a like faithful witness against war from Christians today.

London Yearly Meeting 1900, during the South African War

Meeting at a time when the nations of Europe are engaged in a war of unparalleled magnitude, we have been led to recall the basis of the peace testimony of our religious Society. It is not enough to be satisfied with a barren negative witness, a mere proclamation of non-resistance. We must search for a positive, vital, constructive message. Such a message, a message of supreme love, we find in the life and death of our Lord Jesus Christ. We find it in the doctrine of the indwelling Christ, that re-discovery of the early Friends, leading as it does to a recognition of the brotherhood of all men. Of this doctrine our testimony as to war and peace is a necessary outcome, and if we understand the doctrine aright, and follow it in its wide implications, we shall find that it calls to the peaceable spirit and the rule of love in all the broad and manifold relations of life.

London Yearly Meeting 1915, during the First World War

All thoughtful men and women are torn at heart by the present situation. The savage momentum of war drags us all in its wake. We desire a righteous peace. Yet to attain peace it is claimed that, as Chungking, Rotterdam and Coventry were devastated, so the Eder and Moehne dams must needs be destroyed and whole districts of Hamburg obliterated. The people of Milan and Turin demonstrate for peace but the bombing continues. War is hardening our hearts. To preserve our sanity, we become apathetic. In such an atmosphere no true peace can be framed; yet before us we see months of increasing terror. Can those who pay heed to moral laws, can those who follow Christ submit to the plea that the only way is that demanded by military necessity?

True peace involves freedom from tyranny and a generous tolerance; conditions that are denied over a large part of Europe and are not fulfilled in other parts of the world. But true peace cannot be dictated, it can only be built in co-operation between all peoples. None of us, no nation, no citizen, is free from some responsibility for this situation with its conflicting difficulties.

To the world in its confusion Christ came. Through him we know that God dwells with men and that by turning from evil and living in his spirit we may be led into his way of peace. That way of peace is not to be found in any policy of 'unconditional surrender' by whomsoever demanded. It requires that men and nations should recognise their common brotherhood, using the weapons of integrity, reason, patience and love, never acquiescing in the ways of the oppressor, always ready to suffer with the oppressed.

London Yearly Meeting 1943, during the Second World War

We totally oppose all wars, all preparation for war, all use of weapons and coercion by force, and all military alliances: no end could ever justify such means.

We equally and actively oppose all that leads to violence among people and nations, and violence to other species and to our planet.

Refusal to fight with weapons is not surrender. We are not passive when threatened by the greedy, the cruel, the tyrant, the unjust.

We will struggle to remove the causes of impasse and confrontation by every means of nonviolent resistance available.

We urge all New Zealanders to have the courage to face up to the mess humans are making of our world and to have the faith and diligence to cleanse it and restore the order intended by God.

We must start with our own hearts and minds. Wars will stop only when each of us is convinced that war is never the way.

The places to begin acquiring the skills and maturity and generosity to avoid or to resolve conflicts are in our own homes, our personal relationships, our schools, our workplaces, and wherever decisions are made.

We must relinquish the desire to own other people, to have power over them, and to force our views on to them. We must own up to our own negative side and not look for scapegoats to blame, punish, or exclude. We must resist the urge towards waste and the accumulation of possessions.

Conflicts are inevitable and must not be repressed or ignored but worked through painfully and carefully. We must develop the skills of being sensitive to oppression and grievances, sharing power in decision-making, creating consensus, and making reparation.

What we call for in this statement is a commitment to make the building of peace a priority and to make opposition to war absolute ...

Together, let us reject the clamour of fear and listen to the whisperings of hope.

Yearly Meeting, Aotearoa/New Zealand, 1987

(when many Friends were making submissions to a committee established by their government to review defence policy)

The peace testimony is about deeds not creeds; not a form of words but a

way of living. It is the cumulative lived witness of generations of Quakers
…

The peace testimony is not about being nice to people and living so that everyone likes us. It will remain a stumbling block and will itself cause conflict and disagreement. The peace testimony is a tough demand that we should not automatically accept the categories, definitions and priorities of the world. We look to the Spirit, rather than to prescriptive hypothetical statements.

The peace testimony, today, is seen in what we do, severally and together, with our lives. We pray for the involvement of the Spirit with us, that we may work for a more just world. We need to train to wage peace.

London Yearly Meeting, 1993

Personal testimonies

We had been talking for an hour and a half with a clergyman neighbour, and afterwards I sat by the fire and thought. He had maintained that war has not as yet been grown out of, and that God still uses it as a means of training His children. As I thought over this, old thoughts and memories awoke from sleep. I remembered the familiar words about William Penn's sword – 'Wear it as long as thou canst': and it seemed clear to me that if William Penn had given it up from self-interest or cowardice, or for any reason short of the 'witness of God in his own soul', he would have been wrong. And then the thought extended itself from the life of one man to the life of mankind, and I remembered a sentence in the Epistle to Diognetus: 'What the soul is in the body, that Christians are in the world'. Then I seemed to see that war cannot rightly come to an end from self-interest or cowardice or any worldly reason but only because men and women, by one and one, without waiting for the others, have become loyal to the spirit of Christ.

Marion C Fox, 1914

Compulsory military service was introduced during the two World Wars and Friends, among others, appeared before tribunals to justify their stand as conscientious objectors.

I have sometimes been asked what were my reasons for deciding on that refusal to register for war duties that sent me to Holloway Jail 22 years ago. I can only answer that my reason told me that I was a fool, that I was risking my job and my career, that an isolated example could do no good, that it was a futile gesture since even if I did register my three small children would exempt me. But reason was fighting a losing battle. I had wrestled in prayer and I knew beyond all doubt that I must refuse to register, that those who believed that war was the wrong way to fight evil must stand out against it however much they stood alone, and that I and mine must take the consequences.

The 'and mine' made it more difficult, but I question whether children ever really suffer loss in the long run through having parents who are willing to stand by principles; many a soldier had to leave his family and thought it his duty to do so.

When you have to make a vital decision about behaviour, you cannot sit on the fence. To decide to do nothing is still a decision, and it means that you remain on the station platform or the airstrip when the train or plane has left.

Kathleen Lonsdale, 1964

On my third or fourth attendance at the Sunday service with Friends, an American young Quaker who was on the staff of the American Friends Service Committee working in Tokyo came to talk about his own experiences of having been a conscientious objector during World War II and about the ideas of CO in relation to Quaker beliefs. It really was an epoch-making shock to me to know such a thing as CO existing in this world. I had never heard nor dreamed anything like that even though I had been brought up in a devout Christian family. This person had lived 'love your enemy' in the US at the same time that I had been caught up with the mad notions of nationalism and of winning the 'Holy War' in Japan…

Quaker worship gave me time and space to dissolve my hard shell of self-centredness to be sensitive to discern things with fairness and unaffected by prejudice. I felt the need to be faithful to truth instead of relying on existing judgment. The idea of conscientious objection based on the philosophy of non-violence struck me and was proved to me to be fair, reasonable and Christian. I concluded that it must be the way to take for me and for Japan who had heart-rending experiences of defeat in war and of two nuclear disasters. This became my conviction and I was glad when I realised Japan had declared itself by its new constitution to be a unique CO nation, stating clearly in article 9 of the constitution that it would abolish fighting forces for ever.

One day in Tokyo Local Court, I had an opportunity to make a statement to witness why I felt it necessary to resist tax-payment for military expenditures, saying, 'With military power we cannot protect our life nor keep our human dignity. Even if I should be killed, my way of living or dying to show my sympathy and forgiveness to my opponents, to point to the love of God shown by Jesus Christ on the cross and by his resurrection, will have a better chance to invite others to turn to walk rightly so that we humankind may live together peacefully.'

Susumu Ishitani, 1989

There is hardly a moment when my thoughts are not with the men in France, eager to help the wounded by immediate human touch with their sufferings. This I was privileged to do during nineteen months spent at the

Front with the Friends Ambulance Unit from October 1914 to May 1916, when it was still possible to give voluntary service. At times the impulse to return to this work becomes almost irresistible.

May God steady me, and keep me faithful to a call I have heard above the roar of the guns. By the feverish activity of my hands, I might help to save a fraction of the present human wreckage. That would be for me no sacrifice. It costs far more to spend mind and spirit, if need be, in the silence of a prison cell, in passionate witness for the great truths of Peace.

That is the call I hear.

I believe that only spiritual influence will avail to free the world at last from war, to free the soldiers' little ones and confused struggling humanity itself from all that men and women are suffering now. I honour those who, in loyalty to conscience, have gone out to fight. In a crisis like the present it would be unbecoming to elaborate the reasons which have led me to a course so different. Today a man must act. I believe, with the strength of my whole being, that standing here I am enlisted in active service as a soldier of Jesus Christ, who bids every man be true to the sense of duty that is laid upon his soul.

Corder Catchpool (1883–1952)

(He served in the Friends Ambulance Unit during the First World War, but on the introduction of conscription he returned to England to give his witness as a conscientious objector and was imprisoned for more than two years; later he worked for reconciliation, especially with Germany. The above was what he told the Court Martial which sentenced him at Dovercourt on 28 March 1918)

When I reach heaven's gate, Allah's judgement seat, or whatever you may call it, and there I am asked "What did you do in this life?", am I to say that for the sake of some outside cause I betrayed my own soul?

Words attributed to the Quaker mountaineer "Rick", 1924, conscientious objector in World War II

Now, in the war, I do not think that any of us could doubt the colossal quality of the evil represented by Nazi philosophy. And I do not think that, in political terms, it was possible to contemplate coming to any sort of political compromise with it… Speaking personally as a Christian pacifist, I had a far deeper sense of spiritual unity with those of my friends in the fighting services who, detesting war as deeply as I did, yet felt that there was no other way in which they could share in the agony of the world, than I had with those pacifists who talked as if the suffering of the world could be turned off like a water tap if only politicians would talk sensibly together. Where men have sinned as grievously and as long as we have done in our social and international relations with one another, there can be no easy end to the consequences…

We could not engage in warlike activity in the hope of relieving the suffering of the Jews or of other oppressed peoples in Europe and Asia. We had, somehow, to try to participate in their suffering and to express the conviction that it is ultimately the power of suffering in love that redeems men from the power of evil.

Roger Wilson, 1949

Friends are not naïve enough to believe that such an appeal 'to that of God' in a dictator or in a nation which for psychological or other reasons is in an aggressive mood will necessarily be successful in converting the tyrant or preventing aggression. Christ was crucified; Gandhi was assassinated. Yet they did not fail. Nor did they leave behind them the hatred, devastation and bitterness that war, successful or unsuccessful, does leave. What can be claimed, moreover, is that this method of opposing evil is one of which no person, no group, no nation need be ashamed, as we may and should be ashamed of the inhumanities of war that are perpetrated in our name and with our supports

Kathleen Lonsdale, 1953

Peace begins within ourselves. It is to be implemented within the family, in our meetings, in our work and leisure, in our own localities, and internationally. The task will never be done. Peace is a process to engage in, not a goal to be reached.

Sydney Bailey, 1993

The War Prayer [13]

Mark Twain

The celebrated author Mark Twain wrote this satirical piece in March 1905 and sent it to Harper's Bazaar. They rejected it as too radical—no doubt, like the supposed audience for the prayer, they '"believed that the man was a lunatic ... ".

MarkTwain's piece was published after His death in Harper's Monthly, November 1916.

The satiric tone was well echoed some years later in John Steinbeck's incisive "Short-short story of mankind" [14]

---

[13] Source: https://reasonsforanger.files.wordpress.com/2016/10/warprayer.pdf.

[14] Widely available in the web but the rights holders refuse permission, unless for an immense sum, for its reproduction in hard copy.,

It was a time of great and exalting excitement. The country was up in arms, the war was on, in every breast burned the holy fire of patriotism; the drums were beating, the bands playing, the toy pistols popping, the bunched firecrackers hissing and spluttering; on every hand and far down the receding and fading spread of roofs and balconies a fluttering wilderness of flags flashed in the sun; daily the young volunteers marched down the wide avenue gay and fine in their new uniforms, the proud fathers and mothers and sisters and sweethearts cheering them with voices choked with happy emotion as they swung by; nightly the packed mass meetings listened, panting, to patriot oratory which stirred the deepest deeps of their hearts, and which they interrupted at briefest intervals with cyclones of applause, the tears running down their cheeks the while; in the churches the pastors preached devotion to flag and country, and invoked the God of Battles beseeching His aid in our good cause in outpourings of fervid eloquence which moved every listener. It was indeed a glad and gracious time, and the half dozen rash spirits that ventured to disapprove of the war and cast a doubt upon its righteousness straightway got such a stern and angry warning that for their personal safety's sake they quickly shrank out of sight and offended no more in that way.

Sunday morning came—next day the battalions would leave for the front; the church was filled; the volunteers were there, their young faces alight with martial dreams—visions of the stern advance, the gathering momentum, the rushing charge, the flashing sabres, the flight of the foe, the tumult, the enveloping smoke, the fierce pursuit, the surrender! Then home from the war, bronzed heroes, welcomed, adored, submerged in golden seas of glory! With the volunteers sat their dear ones, proud, happy, and envied by the neighbours and friends who had no sons and brothers to send forth to the field of honor, there to win for the flag, or, failing, die the noblest of noble deaths. The service proceeded; a war chapter from the Old Testament was read; the first prayer was said; it was followed by an organ burst that shook the building, and with one impulse the house rose, with glowing eyes and beating hearts, and poured out that tremendous invocation

> *God the all-terrible! Thou who ordainest! Thunder thy clarion and lightning thy sword!*

Then came the "long'" prayer. None could remember the like of it for passionate pleading and moving and beautiful language. The burden of its supplication was, that an ever-merciful and benignant Father of us all would watch over our noble young soldiers, and aid, comfort, and encourage them in their patriotic work; bless them, shield them in the day of battle and the hour of peril, bear them in His mighty hand, make them strong and confident, invincible in the bloody onset; help them to crush the foe, grant to them and to their flag and country imperishable honour and glory—

An aged stranger entered and moved with slow and noiseless step up the main aisle, his eyes fixed upon the minister, his long body clothed in a robe that reached to his feet, his head bare, his white hair descending in a frothy cataract to his shoulders, his seamy face unnaturally pale, pale even to ghastliness. With all eyes following him and wondering, he made his silent way; without pausing, he ascended to the preacher's side and stood there waiting. With shut lids the preacher, unconscious of his presence, continued with his moving prayer, and at last finished it with the words, uttered in fervent appeal, "Bless our arms, grant us the victory, O Lord our God, Father and Protector of our land and flag!"

The stranger touched his arm, motioned him to step aside—which the startled minister did—and took his place. During some moments he surveyed the spellbound audience with solemn eyes, in which burned an uncanny light; then in a deep voice he said:

"I come from the Throne—bearing a message from Almighty God!' The words smote the house with a shock; if the stranger perceived it he gave no attention. 'He has heard the prayer of His servant your shepherd, and will grant it if such shall be your desire after I, His messenger, shall have explained to you its import— that is to say, its full import. For it is like unto many of the prayers of men, in that it asks for more than he who utters it is aware of—except he pause and think.

"God's servant and yours has prayed his prayer. Has he paused and taken thought? Is it one prayer? No, it is two—one uttered, the other not. Both have reached the ear of Him Who heareth all supplications, the spoken and the unspoken. Ponder this—keep it in mind. If you would beseech a blessing upon yourself, beware! lest without intent you invoke a curse upon a neighbour at the same time. If you pray for the blessing of rain upon your crop which needs it, by that act you are possibly praying for a curse upon some neighbour's crop which may not need rain and can be injured by it.

"You have heard your servant's prayer—the uttered part of it. I am commissioned of God to put into words the other part of it—that part which the pastor—and also you in your hearts—fervently prayed silently. And ignorantly and unthinkingly? God grant that it was so! You heard these words: 'Grant us the victory, O Lord our God!' That is sufficient. *The whole* of the uttered prayer is compact into those pregnant words. Elaborations were not necessary. When you have prayed for victory you have prayed for many unmentioned results which follow victory—*must* follow it, cannot help but follow it. Upon the listening spirit of God fell also the unspoken part of the prayer. He commandeth me to put it into words. Listen!

"O Lord our Father, our young patriots, idols of our hearts, go forth to battle—be Thou near them! With them—in spirit—we also go forth from the sweet peace of our beloved firesides to smite the foe. O Lord our God, help us to tear their soldiers to bloody shreds with our shells; help us to cover their smiling fields with the pale forms of their patriot dead; help us to drown the thunder of the guns with the shrieks of their wounded, writhing in pain; help us to lay waste their humble homes with a hurricane of fire; help us to wring the hearts of their unoffending widows with unavailing grief; help us to turn them out roofless with little children to wander unfriended the wastes of their desolated land in rags and hunger and thirst, sports of the sun flames of summer and the icy winds of winter, broken in spirit, worn with travail, imploring Thee for the refuge of the grave and denied it—for our sakes who adore Thee, Lord, blast their hopes, blight their lives, protract their bitter pilgrimage, make heavy their steps, water their way with their tears, stain the white snow with the blood of their wounded feet! We ask it, in the spirit of love, of Him Who is the Source of Love, and Who is the ever-faithful refuge and friend of all that are sore beset and seek His aid with humble and contrite hearts. Amen."

(*After a pause.*) "Ye have prayed it; if ye still desire it, speak! The messenger of the Most High waits!"

It was believed afterward that the man was a lunatic, because there was no sense in what he said.

The way of peace [15]

James Allen

James Allen (1864-1912) was born in Leicester, England, of working class parents, obliged from an early age to work to support his family. He eventually became an influential philosopher, one of the "New Thought - Ancient Wisdom" movement at the turn of the century. He was also a pioneer of self-help writings (the most famous being As a man liveth). *These sold in huge numbers at the time and several are still in print.*

... "There is an inmost centre in us all
Where Truth abides in fulness; and around,
Wall upon wall, the gross flesh hems it in;
This perfect, clear perception, which is Truth,
A baffling and perverting carnal mesh
Blinds it, and makes all error; and to know,
Rather consists in opening out a way
Whence the imprisoned splendour may escape,
Than in effecting entry for a light
Supposed to be without." ....

Great glory crowns the heights of hope by arduous struggle won;
Bright honor rounds the hoary head that mighty works hath done;
Fair riches come to him who strives in ways of golden gain.
And fame enshrines his name who works with genius-glowing brain;
But greater glory waits for him who, in the bloodless strife
'Gainst self and wrong, adopts, in love, the sacrificial life;
And brighter honor rounds the brow of him who, 'mid the scorns
Of blind idolaters of self, accepts the crown of thorns;
And fairer purer riches come to him who greatly strives
To walk in ways of love and truth to sweeten human lives;
And he who serveth well mankind exchanges fleeting fame
For Light eternal, Joy and Peace, and robes of heavenly flame ...

The realization of perfect peace

In the external universe there is ceaseless turmoil, change, and unrest; at the heart of all things there is undisturbed repose; in this deep silence dwelleth the Eternal.

Man partakes of this duality, and both the surface change and disquietude, and the deep-seated eternal abode of Peace, are contained

---

[15] *Source: from http://www.gutenberg.org/files/10740/10740-8.txt/ (accessesd April 2017).*

within him.

As there are silent depths in the ocean which the fiercest storm cannot reach, so there are silent, holy depths in the heart of man which the storms of sin and sorrow can never disturb. To reach this silence and to live consciously in it is peace.

Discord is rife in the outward world, but unbroken harmony holds sway at the heart of the universe. The human soul, torn by discordant passion and grief, reaches blindly toward the harmony of the sinless state, and to reach this state and to live consciously in it is peace.

Hatred severs human lives, fosters persecution, and hurls nations into ruthless war, yet men, though they do not understand why, retain some measure of faith in the overshadowing of a Perfect Love; and to reach this Love and to live consciously in it is peace.

And this inward peace, this silence, this harmony, this Love, is the Kingdom of Heaven, which is so difficult to reach because few are willing to give up themselves and to become as little children.

> "Heaven's gate is very narrow and minute,
> It cannot be perceived by foolish men
> Blinded by vain illusions of the world;
> E'en the clear-sighted who discern the way,
> And seek to enter, find the portal barred,
> And hard to be unlocked. Its massive bolts
> Are pride and passion, avarice and lust."

Men cry peace! peace! where there is no peace, but on the contrary, discord, disquietude and strife. Apart from that Wisdom which is inseparable from self-renunciation, there can be no real and abiding peace.

The peace which results from social comfort, passing gratification, or worldly victory is transitory in its nature, and is burnt up in the heat of fiery trial. Only the Peace of Heaven endures through all trial, and only the selfless heart can know the Peace of Heaven.

Holiness alone is undying peace. Self-control leads to it, and the ever-increasing Light of Wisdom guides the pilgrim on his way. It is partaken of in a measure as soon as the path of virtue is entered upon, but it is only realized in its fullness when self disappears in the consummation of a stainless life.

> "This is peace,
> To conquer love of self and lust of life,

> To tear deep-rooted passion from the heart
> To still the inward strife."

O reader! you would realize the Light that never fades, the Joy that never ends, and the tranquillity that cannot be disturbed; if you would leave behind for ever your sins, your sorrows, your anxieties and perplexities; if, I say, you would partake of this salvation, this supremely glorious Life, then conquer yourself. Bring every thought, every impulse, every desire into perfect obedience to the divine power resident within you. There is no other way to peace but this, and if you refuse to walk it, your much praying and your strict adherence to ritual will be fruitless and unavailing, and neither gods nor angels can help you. Only to him that overcometh is given the white stone of the regenerate life, on which is written the New and Ineffable Name.

Come away, for awhile, from external things, from the pleasures of the senses, from the arguments of the intellect, from the noise and the excitements of the world, and withdraw yourself into the inmost chamber of your heart, and there, free from the sacrilegious intrusion of all selfish desires, you will find a deep silence, a holy calm, a blissful repose, and if you will rest awhile in that holy place, and will meditate there, the faultless eye of Truth will open within you, and you will see things as they really are. This holy place within you is your real and eternal self; it is the divine within you; and only when you identify yourself with it can you be said to be "clothed and in your right mind." It is the abode of peace, the temple of wisdom, the dwelling-place of immortality. Apart from this inward resting-place, this Mount of Vision, there can be no true peace, no knowledge of the Divine, and if you can remain there for one minute, one hour, or one day, it is possible for you to remain there always. All your sins and sorrows, your fears and anxieties are your own, and you can cling to them or you can give them up. Of your own accord you cling to your unrest; of your own accord you can come to abiding peace. No one else can give up sin for you; you must give it up yourself. The greatest teacher can do no more than walk the way of Truth for himself, and point it out to you; you yourself must walk it for yourself. You can obtain freedom and peace alone by your own efforts, by yielding up that which binds the soul, and which is destructive of peace.

The angels of divine peace and joy are always at hand, and if you do not see them, and hear them, and dwell with them, it is because you shut yourself out from them, and prefer the company of the spirits of evil within you. You are what you will to be, what you wish to be, what you prefer to be. You can commence to purify yourself, and by so doing can arrive at peace, or you can refuse to purify yourself, and so remain with suffering.

Step aside, then; come out of the fret and the fever of life; away from the scorching heat of self, and enter the inward resting-place where the cooling airs of peace will calm, renew, and restore you.

Come out of the storms of sin and anguish. Why be troubled and tempest-tossed when the haven of Peace of God is yours!

Give up all self-seeking; give up self, and lo! the Peace of God is yours!

Subdue the animal within you; conquer every selfish uprising, every discordant voice; transmute the base metals of your selfish nature into the unalloyed gold of Love, and you shall realize the Life of Perfect Peace. Thus subduing, thus conquering, thus transmuting, you will, O reader! while living in the flesh, cross the dark waters of mortality, and will reach that Shore upon which the storms of sorrow never beat, and where sin and suffering and dark uncertainty cannot come. Standing upon that Shore, holy, compassionate, awakened, and self-possessed and glad with unending gladness, you will realize that

"Never the Spirit was born, the Spirit will cease to be never;
Never was time it was not, end and beginning are dreams;
Birthless and deathless and changeless remaineth the Spirit for ever;
Death hath not touched it at all, dead though the house of it seems."

You will then know the meaning of Sin, of Sorrow, of Suffering, and that the end thereof is Wisdom; will know the cause and the issue of existence.

And with this realization you will enter into rest, for this is the bliss of immortality, this the unchangeable gladness, this the untrammeled knowledge, undefiled Wisdom, and undying Love; this, and this only, is the realization of Perfect Peace.

   O thou who wouldst teach men of Truth!
     Hast thou passed through the desert of doubt?
   Art thou purged by the fires of sorrow? hath ruth
       The fiends of opinion cast out
   Of thy human heart? Is thy soul so fair
   That no false thought can ever harbor there?
   O thou who wouldst teach men of Love!
     Hast thou passed through the place of despair?
     Hast thou wept through the dark night of grief?
     does it move (now freed from its sorrow and care)
   Thy human heart to pitying gentleness,
   Looking on wrong, and hate, and ceaseless stress?
   O thou who wouldst teach men of Peace!
     Hast thou crossed the wide ocean of strife?
   Hast thou found on the Shores of the Silence,
       Release from all the wild unrest of life?

From thy human heart hath all striving gone,
Leaving but Truth, and Love, and Peace alone?

The eternal reciprocity of tears [16]
Soldier-poets of the 'Great War'

War poems, above all those from the very field of battle, touch our hearts. There is no time in which such poets are not needed—and come forward-- to speak of the luxury of "peace" and of the horrors and aspirations of war.

Here we have not just the rightly famous poetry of Wilfred Owen but, less known, Gréagóir Ó Dúill's poem in honour of the Irishmen who fought and, in large numbers, died in the "Great" War ("Great" …), now a hundred years ago – and we still continue.

There are also, selected here, the striking poems by those from the German ranks, inexplicably overlooked by English speakers - but perhaps only too explicably as the victors' voice, as ever, prevails.

So, to mention just one, in Emmanuel Saul's incredibly moving words in his long poem about, we have Germany's "holy war" to defend the values of their precious culture.

The poems throw fresh light on the feelings and visions of those on the "other" side.

In memory of 75,000 Irishmen
A mustard miasma rises from trenches,
young officers hurry us onward,
rats from the drains of home when the flood starts
driven on to the metal madness of shells and machine guns.

Clumsy khaki bags in holes
and on the Monday wire washing lines clothes hang.
Soft, softer our bright skin under the raping steel,
a long time amidst crazy screaming, pumping
like arterial blood from a stump.

With lung-rotting gas, mask and bayonet they come tomorrow.
The wire not likely to stop them at rifle range.
Don't ask if this is necessary or right,
that blind bitch appoints the generals.

Deaf to the bells of the Western Island
I will leave this filthy place
lost but alive on the continent

---

[16] *Various sources, available on internet.*

where I will live as a rat, the young officer's body
with a new mouth in his forehead to encourage fools,
a third eye on his bloody brow
to judge angle and deflection,
his body matter to the Easter Fires,
to the Resurrection.
    Gréagóir Ó Dúill) translated by the author from his original Irish

From the *German side*

To my children
When I left home to fight for Fatherland
Against the threat of danger and deceit
You, children, happily around me ran
Rejoicing in your father's bravery,
His uniform and other warlike clothes,
And in his newfound worth and bravery.
All hid from child-like sight was what it means
When now your father leaves for war and death.

But later when you are mature and wise,
And when perhaps my bones far east may lie
Bleaching alone under a wooden cross –
Then dread and horror you may start to feel
And you will think about that far-off time
When we all said farewell for the last time.
The certainty will ease your private pain
That proud and joyful he did join the ranks
Who all fought for our Reich's security.

And do you want to know why I went out,
Enthused and happy joining all the rest,
My life by sweetest wife and love still crowned,
While you in childhood's blossom sweet and pure
Appeared before me in your beauteous youth?

I say to you, and listen carefully
I left you all because a German I,
No other way could I think, feel or act!
A German in each fibre of my heart.
Strong feelings as a student came to me
Of noble, precious German worth and good.
My childish heart rejoiced when I did hear
Of German victories and greatness told.

But when each sudden blow my nation struck,
It shattered me deep in my inmost soul;

It penetrated me so deep in marrow's core
That it became my life's experience.

So moved was I deep in my heart of hearts
Because of tragic destiny that struck
And tried to kill the noble dynasty
The kingly breed of Hohenstauffens proud,

So deeply moved was I that, yet a child,
Still tied to school desk and not yet mature
It held the grip of written fantasy.

Then came a war with German forces strong
Not only against German pride and power –
But against German peoples, German kind,
Consciously evil, devilishly conceived –
A war, not fought as knights with weapon bared,
But hunger's ruin forcing us to yield.
With bold lies and the basest treachery
With despicable and immoral acts
They wanted to destroy our long-sought peace
Achieved by German peoples' work and toil.
The blooming of our scientists' research
Creations of our keen artistic Volk
The blessings of our culture most refined
The glorious and proud acts of German spirits
The sound of German poetry and bloom
Of happy lives created by hard work
The blessings of our work with brother's hands
In company with values strong and good.

Yes, snuffed out and destroyed, removed from life
A world without our art they wished to see!

It is a war, heart beating strong in breast
With mindful thoughts and blood strong in the veins,
Proclaimed against a hellish evil beast.
And to what end? The merchants to enrich
And thieves hungry for gold to make more rich.
And then our holy anger was enflamed:
How else could I have thought and felt right then
When German nation's brave and brightest youth,

When I too loved our holy German art?
Could outrage not then fill my deepest soul
When German essence is now so defiled
When we are blamed for all outrageous acts

When slanderous doubts of our nobility
Drag us all down in mud and dirt and filth.

Relief and not complaint rose in my soul
When fate chose me for battle's severe test,
Vengeance to take on malice, lies, deceit
Defending German richness and fair bloom,
To fight for wife and child for my land's sake,
Protecting them from Asiatic hordes,
That breed of tigers at our eastern gate
Who heinously with us in past has dealt.

What noble joy! Thus did I leave with hope,
A German, German borders to protect –

And yet another thing drove me to war.
I am a Jew, and faithful, true and proud
Of the tribe from whose blood I take my source.
In time of peace we oft are spoken of
With calumny about our Jewish faith.
We are called base cowards unfit to fight
And turned away from lofty goals of life,
Mean, low and selfish, gain-obsessed,
They curse us cruelly – and this is the worst
The hard blow that strikes like the whip's lash –
As foreign on the soil for which our fathers
Have paid both with their sweat and with their blood. –

My heart is now gripped with time's urgency
One will have I, one single holy wish
That Jew and German bind themselves as one.
That we are German needs no outside proof,
The truth thereof shines clearly as the sun,
We Jews all leave for war of our own wish,
Joyful to throng around our country's flag
To gain for ourselves – even if fate wills
That we pay with our blood – our Fatherland.

For Jewish kin have sadly called the land
In which we live Stepfatherland:
This was my last but well-considered wish....
That I and all of us will prove our strength:
Our Fatherland for which we have such love
That placed us at the back unjustly, wrong
And that we fight bravely when duty calls
To strike the foe like, once in days of yore,
The Maccabees, proud scions of our tribe -

Who are our enemies in this just war,

The Judas, old notorious foe of yore
The cruel old oppressor of our race,
The enemies of culture, freedom, right,
Who are our enemies now? – One hate
Unites us, finally, with freedom's joy
Warriors for culture, German, Jew unite
And then will bloom one common destiny:

Defeat may lead to our destruction, sure,
But victory frees, ennobles, gives us joy.
For what can we expect from our cruel foe,
That now spills Jewish blood in their own lands,
Flowing in streams, and causes grief and woe
To Jewish children, women without fault?

Therefore I left for battle, as I am.
A German Jew to fight in holy war.

            Emmanuel Saul

To a missing friend
You have no grave, no cross … but you did die.
Maybe in some dark thicket your bones lie
Or you were sunk in swamp in deep of night,
Or Cossacks cruelly robbed you of the light.

And when it was and where and how …and why
I know not: death in forest does not cry.
You are a skull now white-bleached by the rain
Round which the weasel lightly leaves its train.

You are the ploughed earth on which horses stand
You are the grain that once did crown the land
You are the bread the farmer once did eat
You are the strength when peace returns to greet.
  "Goldfield" (killed during the war; no more is known about him,
            not even his first name)

Sounds of Elull
A black and rainy evening
With vague feelings of fear
Alive with garish shrieking
Of shots both far and near.

What bring you, laughing soldier
To my heart's dark command

When I, pensive and sober,
In my own grave do stand

What strange column unmoving
Appears with such dark dread?
-- Oh, friends you are still living! --
Death, is your realm not fed?

At home with pious greeting
Loved ones the graves do search
Where are the dead now meeting?
The wind blows o'er the church

Death touches grave and heather
And sings: "This have I done."
Perhaps from my eyes forever
Night will now hide the sun.

    Robert Ziegel (Ellul is the Hebrew month preceding the High
                Holiday autumn season)

Out of the trenches: the brothers
The man has submerged in the great army;
The army has disappeared into the earth; far away lies the sea
Of night-covered forest chains.
Lost breezes pass between home and enemy land,
They meet and fade away.
And patrols rise up from the trenches like ghosts from the grave
A helmet appears large for a moment before the night sky.
Then the whispering troop disappears in the stormy woods.
Only the wind rustles in the tree-tops and a call echoes in the darkness.

Patrol meets patrols and stamps like shadows past each another
And one recognizes, from a voice in the dark, his brother and like a choked cry
Whispers are heard as they pass:
Wilhelm? Heinrich? Mother wrote today?.
"Greetings" Till we meet again!"
And then they disappear in different directions in the darkness.

The forest paths gleam brightly lit broadly by a flare
Again sunken in the night: shots from the forward posts
Silence of the hostile world.

                     Leo Sternberg

Out of the trenches: the relief
We lie snowed in the trenches like snow-covered clods of earth,

Unknowing mirrors of the days and nights that roll over us,
In the foremost trenches, cut off from the help of the world
In front of the gun barrels of the enemies who aim across the level field,
Our breasts, like our raised earth wall, only a defense
Our death cry only a signal for the army
Behind us, We are only the feelers and the nerve cord
On which the burning town in the night and the flare pistols play their song
Every whispered word, heard at the front
Every step, that hisses in the trenches before us
Until the hour of relief nears, when suddenly out of the foggy night
An unknown person stirs us, who will watch for us and continue the fight.
And we reach our comrade, whom we do not see.
Through the fog we grasp his hand and take up the rifle and start to go.
Then before we leave our post,
A bullet lies before us in the snowy clods atop the trenches edge.

Leo Sternberg

Prayer before battle
*(*The soldiers pray fervently, every man for himself)

God, protect me from bad luck.
Father, son and holy ghost,
Please don't let any shells hit me,
Or those scoundrels, our enemies
Imprison or shoot me,
Don't let me kick the bucket like a dog
For the dear Fatherland.

See, I would like to still live
Milk cows, bang girls,
And beat up that rascal, Sepp.
And get boozed up many times
Before I meet my holy end.

See, I'll pray well and willingly
Say seven rosaries daily,
If, God, in your mercy
You kill my friends Huber or Meier
But spare me.

But if I've got to take it
Let me not be wounded too heavily.
Send me a light leg-wound,

A small arm injury,
So that I return home as a hero
Who can tell many a story.

                              Alfred Lichtenstein

Romantic journey
A thousand stars are shining in the heaven
The landscape shines, and from the far-off meadows
The human marching column slowly nears.
Just once it is detached – and, lost in thought --
A young lieutenant, a page-boy in love.
But finally combat wagons start to move.
The moon makes this all look particular.
And now and then the drivers shout out loud:
Halt!

High on the wobbliest cartridge wagon sits
Like a small fiery toad, refinely carved
From blackest wood, his hands balled lightly closed,
His rifle on his back, sword buckled light,
A large smoking cigar in crooked mouth
Monk-lazy, full of longing like a dog
Valerian drops pressed tightly to his heart –
Old-funny, mad, serious, with yellowed mouth:
Kuno.
        Alfred Lichtenstein (Kuno was one of Lichtenstein's comrades)

Corpses in the woods
A dung heap of rotting corpses:
Glazed eyes, bloodshot,
Brains split, guts spewed out
The air poisoned by the stink of corpses
A single awful cry of madness

Oh women of France,
Women of Germany
Regard your menfolk!
They fumble with torn hands
For the swollen bodies of their enemies,
Gestures, stiff in death, become the touch of brotherhood,
Yes they embrace each other,
Oh, horrible embrace!

I see and see and am struck dumb
Am I a beast, a murderous dog?
Men violated….
Murdered….

Ernst Toller

Nightmare
On a pole, rotten and foul
Squats the conscience of nations,
Three childrens' bones dance around the pole
Broken from a young mother's body.
A sheep bleats the rhythm bäh bäh.

Ernst Toller

From the English side

This is no case of petty right or wrong
This is no case of petty right or wrong
That politicians or philosophers
Can judge. I hate not Germans, nor grow hot
With love of Englishmen, to please newspapers.
Beside my hate for one fat patriot
My hatred of the Kaiser is love true: –
A kind of god he is, banging a gong.
But I have not to choose between the two,
Or between justice and injustice. Dinned
With war and argument I read no more
Than in the storm smoking along the wind
Athwart1 the wood. Two witches' cauldrons roar.
From one the weather shall rise clear and gay;
Out of the other an England beautiful
And like her mother that died yesterday.
Little I know or care if, being dull,
I shall miss something that historians
Can rake out of the ashes when perchance2
The phoenix3 broods serene above their ken.
But with the best and meanest Englishmen
I am one in crying, God save England, lest
We lose what never slaves and cattle blessed.
The ages made her that made us from dust:
She is all we know and live by, and we trust
She is good and must endure, loving her so:
And as we love ourselves we hate her foe.
Edward Thomas (written 26 December 1915 after a blazing row
with his father, a conventional patriot
who demonised the Germans)

Here dead we lie
Here dead we lie
Because we did not choose

To live and shame the land
From which we sprung.

Life, to be sure,
Is nothing much to lose,
But young men think it is,
And we were young.

A.E. Housman

Poems from Wilfred Owen's "Apologia pro poem ate meo"

I, too, saw God through mud—
   The mud that cracked on cheeks when wretches smiled.
   War brought more glory to their eyes than blood,
   And gave their laughs more glee than shakes a child.

Merry it was to laugh there—
   Where death becomes absurd and life absurder.
   For power was on us as we slashed bones bare
   Not to feel sickness or remorse of murder.

I, too, have dropped off fear—
   Behind the barrage, dead as my platoon,
   And sailed my spirit surging, light and clear
   Past the entanglement where hopes lay strewn;

And witnessed exultation—
   Faces that used to curse me, scowl for scowl,
   Shine and lift up with passion of oblation,
   Seraphic for an hour; though they were foul.

I have made fellowships—
   Untold of happy lovers in old song.
   For love is not the binding of fair lips
   With the soft silk of eyes that look and long,

By Joy, whose ribbon slips,—
   But wound with war's hard wire whose stakes are strong;
   Bound with the bandage of the arm that drips;
   Knit in the welding of the rifle-thong.

I have perceived much beauty
   In the hoarse oaths that kept our courage straight;
   Heard music in the silentness of duty;
   Found peace where shell-storms spouted reddest spate.

Nevertheless, except you share
   With them in hell the sorrowful dark of hell,

Whose world is but the trembling of a flare,
And heaven but as the highway for a shell,

You shall not hear their mirth:
   You shall not come to think them well content
   By any jest of mine. These men are worth
   Your tears: You are not worth their merriment.

Anthem for Doomed Youth

What passing-bells for these who die as cattle?
   Only the monstrous anger of the guns.
   Only the stuttering rifles' rapid rattle
Can patter out their hasty orisons.
No mockeries for them; no prayers nor bells,
Nor any voice of mourning save the choirs,—
The shrill, demented choirs of wailing shells;
And bugles calling for them from sad shires.

What candles may be held to speed them all?
   Not in the hands of boys, but in their eyes
Shall shine the holy glimmers of goodbyes.
   The pallor of girls' brows shall be their pall;
Their flowers the tenderness of patient minds,
And each slow dusk a drawing-down of blinds.

Insensibility
Happy are men who yet before they are killed
Can let their veins run cold.
Whom no compassion fleers
Or makes their feet
Sore on the alleys cobbled with their brothers.
The front line withers,
But they are troops who fade, not flowers
For poets' tearful fooling:
Men, gaps for filling
Losses who might have fought
Longer; but no one bothers.

And some cease feeling
Even themselves or for themselves.
Dullness best solves
The tease and doubt of shelling,
And Chance's strange arithmetic
Comes simpler than the reckoning of their shilling.
They keep no check on Armies' decimation.

Happy are these who lose imagination:
They have enough to carry with ammunition.
Their spirit drags no pack.
Their old wounds save with cold can not more ache.
Having seen all things red,
Their eyes are rid
Of the hurt of the colour of blood for ever.
And terror's first constriction over,
Their hearts remain small drawn.
Their senses in some scorching cautery of battle
Now long since ironed,
Can laugh among the dying, unconcerned.

Happy the soldier home, with not a notion
How somewhere, every dawn, some men attack,
And many sighs are drained.
Happy the lad whose mind was never trained:
His days are worth forgetting more than not.
He sings along the march
Which we march taciturn, because of dusk,
The long, forlorn, relentless trend
From larger day to huger night.

We wise, who with a thought besmirch
Blood over all our soul,
How should we see our task
But through his blunt and lashless eyes?
Alive, he is not vital overmuch;
Dying, not mortal overmuch;
Nor sad, nor proud,
Nor curious at all.
He cannot tell
Old men's placidity from his.

But cursed are dullards whom no cannon stuns,
That they should be as stones.
Wretched are they, and mean
With paucity that never was simplicity.
By choice they made themselves immune
To pity and whatever mourns in man
Before the last sea and the hapless stars;
Whatever mourns when many leave these shores;
Whatever shares
The eternal reciprocity of tears.

War at any price? [17]

Tom Finnegan

This thoughtful and knowledgeable treatment was published privately in Northern Ireland as a modest pamphlet, reflecting both fears of the possible war to come and memories of the previous one.

Both Tom and his brother Robert (killed driving an ambulance in the closing weeks of the first war) had been brought up in Belfast in, unusually for their time, a German-speaking family, part of the background, together with his brother's fate, for the author's lifelong pacifism. In both this and his love for the German people and culture he was soon joined and encouraged by his wife-to-be, Agnes Campbell, and by other members of the peace movement of the time.

For their efforts to rescue Austrian Jews and give them a home in Ulster, and for their lifelong efforts to bring about peace and reconciliation both locally and worldwide, Tom and his wife were reviled locally as "Nazi-lovers'"!) and rebels. Some years later they were, as a result, in effect driven out of Northern Ireland.

The pamphlet is addressed to the great and increasing number of people who are seriously perplexed about the question of war and peace, who look with apprehension at the present re-armament programme and who yet feel that as other nations are doing the same thing there is no alternative for a nation like Great Britain which has so vas t commitments all over the world. But they see too that this course is most likely to lead to disaster in the end and not least for our own country.

In their perplexity they ask the pacifists, on the one hand, what is to be done in the face of the aggression of Mussolini, the Japanese and Franco, and in face of the threats of Hitler. On the other hand, they ask the militarists whether the methods of modern warfare can defend any principles without at the same time violating others jus t as important, for the most clear-sighted at least see that the methods of modern war involve the bombing of civilian populations from the air, the wholesale slaughter of innocent people, particularly of women and children, for once a war has started these things will be done by every nation. Are not such methods, it is asked, a wasteful and inefficient method of resistance, which merely makes a desolation and calls it peace?

These are questions to which answers must be given by any serious searcher for truth, and I hope in this pamphlet to make clear the lines

---

[17] *Abridged from Tom Finnegan's booklet of that title, published locally in 1937.*

along which I believe they can be answered. I have myself after much difficult questioning arrived at the pacifist position. I avoided it as long as I could, for apart from any other consideration it is never easy to differ from so many people on a question which arouses so deep and genuine feelings in those who take an opposite view. But 1 think that I can fairly claim to have given full consideration to the militarist point of view: I even underwent three years' military training in a Senior I division Officers' Training Corps. In the pacifism which I am here putting forward many of the best qualities of the soldier will be needed—self-sacrifice, discipline, physical fitness, and courage.

I have felt for some time past that my views on peace and war have been the subject of much adverse criticism. Part of the cause of this has been, I believe, that I have never had the opportunity of putting as fully as I should have liked the case for pacifism. I could not hope that this pamphlet will cause all criticism to cease, but perhaps I may venture to hope that it will lead some to realise that the position is not al together unreasonable. If I can persuade some to agree with me, so much the better.

Facing facts.
For some years before 1914, the world witnessed a feverish armaments race between two groups of powers and mainly between Britain and Germany for naval supremacy. The balance of power in Europe was held by two blocks of powers which when the moment arrived came into conflict. The aims of those who fought were on each side claimed to be honourable—on the German side, the soldier fought to give his country room to expand (for this seemed necessary), to prevent its encirclement by a group of hostile powers, on the Allied side the declared aims were to make the world safe for democracy, to make defence against tyranny, to s tamp out militarism, and, as the conflict lengthened and the horrors of war became more and more realised, to fight a war to end war.

The Allied side won and the harshest terms possible were imposed on the conquered, so presumably the Allied aims were achieved. But were they? Militarism is now more widespread than in 1914 and not only in Germany. Two of the countries, Italy and Japan, which fought on the Allied side are now leaders in aggressive militarism. And the same two countries far from making the world safe for democracy glory in their rejection of it, and far from showing a desire to end war have been responsible for the starting of two new ones.

And further, these developments can be traced almost directly to the Great War itself and to the treaties of peace imposed after it. The cost of the Great War, which thus so signally failed to achieve the ends of either side engaged in it has been reckoned at eighty thousand million pounds. This sum would have sufficed to provide every family in America, Canada,

Australia, Great Britain and Ireland, France, Belgium, Germany and Russia with a five-hundred pound house, two hundred pounds worth of furniture, and a hundred pounds worth of land. Every town of twenty thousand inhabitants and over in all the above-mentioned countries, could have been presented with a library to the value of a million pounds and a university to the value of two millions. After which it would have been possible to buy the whole of France and Belgium, that is, all the land, houses, factories, railways, churches, roads, harbours, etc., in these countries. This means that, with the money required to impose the Treaty of Versailles on Germany, one could have bought lock, stock and barrel, five countries as large as France and five others as large as Belgium. To impose the Britain of Versailles thirteen millions of human beings were killed outright, while war conditions were responsible for the death of many millions more.

By the peace treaties Germany was deprived of her colonial possessions, and she was forced to pay a vast sum in reparations. Her confiscated colonies were handed over to the control of the League of Nations through the Mandate system, but only the powers of the Allied side were given any mandates. It is illuminating to look at the facts about the distribution of mandates. Fourteen mandates were assigned to different countries under the Versailles Treaty. Japan was given one, Belgium one, France three, British Empire nine, Italy none.

These facts partly at least explain the present world situation. We see in the world to-day two main groups of nations (a) the satisfied, and (b) the dissatisfied. The satisfied nations are Britain, France, U.S.A., Russia, along with such small nations as Denmark, Norway and Sweden. The dissatisfied nations are Japan, Germany and Italy. And it is from these dissatisfied nations that at the moment the threat to peace comes. The satisfied nations have got all they want and they show no inclination to give up any of their privileges.

The dissatisfied nations declare that their dissatisfaction is due to their exclusion from privilege and in particular from the alleged advantages of colonial possessions. As a result of a series of international blunders for which it is not necessary at this stage to assign responsibility but which might perhaps have been avoided, the nations are now busily carrying out programmes of rearmament. No large measure of agreement seems to have been reached even by League members to adjust their rearmament to the requirements of collective security, each nation in effect returning to the policy of making itself safe without reference to others.

Great Britain like the rest has entered on this mad career. Because other nations arc mad, she must needs be mad too, it is argued. Earl Baldwin at the Lord Mayor's banquet on November 9th, 1936, said:

'The whole of Europe is arming—an inconceivable folly for those of us who have the responsibility of governing the great countries of Europe. What good can come of it? If armaments continue I don't say they mean war, but they make war more likely. I am prepared to devote all our efforts, whatever it may cost in men and money to do what is necessary, but 1 am conscious all the time of the folly of all of us.'

To which the only reply is that the way to cease from being mad is to be sane, however many other people may be mad. The sane people in this crisis are those who refuse to be infected by the insanity of others.

Let no one delude himself into thinking that we shall not use our force to scatter gas bombs and other kinds of bombs on civilian populations and on open towns.

War cannot now be fought on gentlemanly lines and it is folly to expect it; once a war has started the methods used are determined by our opponents as well as by ourselves. We bombed open towns in the last war and we shall do it in the next—an extraordinary instance of the psychological change that comes over all of us in times of war'.

It is well then to face up to the fact that if we are prepared to wage even a defensive war we are commit ted to the maiming and suffocating and terrorising of innocent men, women and children, and that many of our fittest and best young men must be trained for that purpose. Many may think that this is regrettable but inevitable, but let them not talk in idealistic terms only of men dying for their country, but let them realise that modern war, whatever was the truth about past wars, demands the killing, demands the torture, of civilian populations as well as of combatants. But it is worthwhile to pursue a little farther this subject of defence.

It is clear that in an air raid some bombers at least will get through. Even supposing the objectives of the raid are purely military and not the civilian population, the chief result of the defensive action against the raiding planes by intercepting planes and anti-aircraft guns will be to make them drop their bombs more hurriedly than they otherwise would and therefore not on their objectives but anywhere possible. This will most likely mean destruction for the civil population even if it is not intended.

The question which many of us ask ourselves is: 'Can any principle be upheld by methods of this kind? Are not all the principles which we wish to uphold immediately violated as soon as we consent to take part in such massacres?'

Pacifists have an alternative method which has been proved to work
The methods of violence can be seen, in the case of modern war at least, to lead to chaos. But the case against violence can be put in more general

terms. Aldous Huxley, in his recently published book *Ends and Means* classifies the cases in which victory in war provides a more or less lasting settlement.

(1) Victory results in a lasting settlement when the vanquished are completely or very nearly exterminated, as, for example, when the Red Men in North America were exterminated by the white settlers. But modern wars are generally waged between densely populated countries, and therefore as extermination is unlikely one war tends to beget another.

(2) If the fighting forces are so small that the mass of the rival populations is left physically unharmed and psychologically unembittered by the conflict, victory may result in a permanent settlement. But modem wars are almost certain to involve entire rival populations and therefore this case is not relevant to modern conditions.

(3) Permanent peace may follow victory where the victors settle down among the vanquished and become absorbed by them.

(4) 'Victory may be followed' to use Huxley's own words 'by an act of reparation on the part of the victors. Reparation will disarm the resentment of the vanquished and lead to a permanent settlement. This was the policy pursued by the English after the Boer War. Such a policy is essentially an application of the principles of non-violence. The longer and more savage the conflict, the more difficult is it to make an act of reparation after victory. It was relatively easy for Campbell-Bannerman to be just after the Boer War; for the makers of the Versailles Treaty, magnanimity was psychologically impossible.

In view of this obvious fact, common sense demands that the principles of nonviolence should be applied, not after the war, when their application is supremely difficult, but before physical conflict has broken out and as a substitute for such a conflict. Non-violence is the practical consequence that follows from belief in the fundamental unity of all being.

But, quite apart from the validity of its philosophical basis, non-violence can prove its value pragmatically — by working. That it can work in private life we have all had occasion to observe and experience. We have all seen how anger feeds upon answering anger, but is disarmed by gentleness and patience. We have all known what it is to have our meannesses shamed by somebody else's magnanimity into an equal magnanimity ; what it is to have our dislikes melted away by an act of considerateness; what it is to have our coldnesses and harshnesses transformed into solicitude by the example of another's unselfishness.

The use of violence is accompanied by anger, hatred and fear, or by exultant malice and conscious cruelty. 'Those who would use non-

85

violence must practice self-control, must learn moral as well as physical courage, must pit against anger and malice a steady good will and a patient determination to understand and to sympathise. Violence makes men worse; non-violence makes them better'.

Some modern examples of the success of the method of non-violent resistance.

1. In the middle of the nineteenth century the Emperor Francis Joseph tried to subordinate Hungary to the Austrian power, contrary to the terms of the old treaty of Union between the two countries. Francis Deak, a Catholic landowner of Hungary proceeded to organise resistance to the Austrians along non-violent lines. He proposed a scheme for independent Hungarian education, agriculture and industry, and urged the Hungarians to refuse to recognise the Austrian government in any way and organised a boycott of Austrian goods. He was particularly careful to warn his followers against acts of violence, their case was based on law, and violence would involve the risk of destroying their case.

The Hungarians followed Deak's lead; they refused to pay the Austrian tax-collector, and when the Austrian police seized their goods no Hungarian would auction them and if an Austrian auctioneer was brought no Hungarian would bid.

The Austrians then put in their soldiers. But wherever they were billeted, the Hungarians while not refusing to accept them into their homes, made them feel so despised that the Austrian soldiers made protests to the authorities to be removed. The Austrians declared the boycott illegal but the Hungarians still continued it and the jails were full. Finally the position had been made so difficult for the Austrians that the Emperor eventually capitulated and gave Hungary her constitution.

2. From 1901 to 1905 the Finns conducted a campaign of non-violent resistance to Russian oppression, and in 1905 so successful was the movement that the Russians repealed the law imposing conscription on the Finns.

3. A more important and significant example is to be found in the campaign which began in 1906 in favour of the rights of Indians in South Africa. For many years Indians had been coming to Natal to work in the mines and elsewhere, at first on the invitation of Europeans who wished to use them to develop the country. After some time, however, owing to their industry they began to compete with the Europeans and by 1906 some 12,500 of them had crossed the border into the Transvaal.

In the same year the Government of the Transvaal introduced a bill requiring every Indian to be registered by finger-print, like criminals, and to produce his certificate of registration on the demand of any police officer.

Failure to register meant deportation and refusal to produce the certificate would be punished by fine.

The leading Indians, who had been refused a hearing before the Bill was passed, took an oath that they would all refuse to register and would go to jail rather than obey a law which they felt attacked their religion, their self-respect and their manhood. One of these leading Indians was the now famous M.K. Gandhi, an Indian lawyer trained at an English university. The feeling of injustice was further intensified when the Transvaal Supreme Court made a decision which invalidated all Hindu and Mohammedan marriages, thus rendering all the Indian children illegitimate and incapable of inheriting property.

A large protest march was organised and many were arrested, among whom was Gandhi. The Indians were impounded at the mines and beaten and ill-treated, but they never allowed themselves to be moved from their non-violence. Public opinion was gradually coming over to the side of the Indians, and Lord Hardinge, Viceroy of India, defended the non-violent resisters and criticised severely the acts of the Union of South Africa. In the end the Government was forced to yield and the Indians won the main part of their demands. Their demands therefore were won by non-violent resistance.

4. One further example must suffice. For many years now the North-West Frontier of India has been the scene of repressive warfare on the part of Great Britain. Indeed during the past year £1,000,000 has been spent on this war and 37,000 troops have been engaged. The frontier has always been a source of trouble. No solution seems yet to have been found along military lines. But to find the source of the trouble one must find out the reasons which make men leave their homes and go marauding. For it is only when the root causes are found that the true remedy can be applied.

At least one man has tried this method with success. His name was Dr. Pennell. He was a genius in dealing with the frontier tribesmen:

"He lived among them, adopted their dress, spoke their language fluently, and ultimately laid down his life on their behalf. For he was ministering to a Pathan, who was suffering from plague, when he himself was infected and died of the same disease. I remember well his telling me, with a laugh, the story about how he asked a new commandant for leave to go over the border to heal a sick Pathan. The officer insisted that he should take an escort. Pennell had answered that this was the certain way to get ambushed and shot; but if he went alone he would be perfectly safe. With some difficulty he persuaded the commanding officer and went to the sick man, without any escort, and then returned quite safely as he had often done before.

"Others have told me how a colonel, who knew the frontier well, had said that to have Pennell was worth 'a couple of regiments'—so great a peacemaker had he become. .."

Pennell's one life-aim was to get a series of hospitals, attached to medical missions, stretching across the frontier regions right on up to the untouched lands of Central Asia. He felt certain that such a chain of hospitals would be a potent cause of peace and goodwill and instrumental in aver ting wars and preventing bloodshed.

"I have been," he said on one occasion, "among the fiercest and most fanatical among the tribes across our border. I have never once carried arms, but have wandered alone by day and by night through the frontier country. 1 have lived in their villages, among them, and they have never betrayed me."

If one man could do so much—could be worth 'a couple of regiments'— surely a band of devoted and skilled men could make peace on the frontier, and there would no longer be need for Great Britain to risk the charge of hypocrisy by bombing natives on the North-West Frontier, while expressing horror at the use of bombing methods by other nations.

The way of Dr. Pennell is the way which pacifists suggest, and it is certainly not a policy of 'doing nothing'. Many other examples of this method could be given. The technique required, it is true, is a highly skilled one, but then so is that of the soldier, and there seems no reason why we should not train more and more people in the use of it. The sphere of its use can be more and more enlarged and a start must be made immediately. No one can deny that the method of non-violence may and usually does demand suffering; it will also demand courage, self-discipline, physical fitness, magnanimity and patience.

But it is a way too which is not reserved merely for saints; even quite ordinary people have been shown capable of following it.

Erasmus at the time of the Reformation, led the way, and since his time there have been various Christian groups which have borne their witness for pacifism, most notably the Quakers from the seventeenth century. But the main point is that both the teaching of Jesus, as exemplified particularly in his death, and the teaching of the early Church, seem to stand unequivocally for the pacifist position.

Conclusion
I have tried to show that whatever may have been true of wars in the past, modern methods of war are so destructive that they are ineffective as a means of settling disputes in accordance with any canons of righteousness. They demand such terrible deeds at the hands of those

who are called to take part in war that all principles are violated.

Whatever difficulties there are about the pacifist position, they are not so overwhelming as those of the militarist position, and a pacifist country would at least not be guilty of the provocation due to the possession of an air fleet of which the chief characteristic must be its power of attack.

Further, a truly pacifist position implies positive contributions to peace-making through reconciliation and magnanimity. Great Britain led the world in the abolition of slavery. If she would only lead the world in this colonial question, she would show a like greatness and would earn the admiration of the world, while making a contribution to peace which would be invaluable.

Another question which I can only touch on. It is said that war brings out some of the best qualities in men, courage, self-sacrifice and so on. That, I am the last person to deny.

The trouble is that it brings them out at such a cost. There is, however, a real and legitimate desire on the part, particularly of the young, for adventure, physical danger and the running of risks. That is wholly creditable and must be satisfied. In our social life games satisfy it to some extent but not nearly enough. The method of non-violence may give us as much as we want of that if at any time we have to undertake resistance. But if not we must organise our social life in such a way that those who desire such experiences may get them.

There are plenty of risks which must be run in our social life. It has been suggested that a system of voluntary peace time national service should be organised making it possible for every boy and young man to take his turn at one or other of the tough jobs and civilian risks that exist—fire-brigade service, life-boat service, light-house service, sea fishery, mine safety work, down to traffic direction and sewer inspection. Those whose physique would not permit such roughing could gain as much honour by offering themselves for essential scientific experiments.

In some such way as this, individuals would be given a cause to live for and if necessary to die for—would be enabled to practise the soldier's virtues without committing the crime of war. We would have got a moral equivalent for war.

The final demand upon each one of us is to find peace in our own lives and in our own community. There is little use talking of peace in the larger world if we are still indulging in hat red, anger and greed in our own private lives or in the life of the community in which we live. The only way, in international affairs as well as in personal relationships, is the way of reconciliation, of willingness to seek solution of conflicts in fair discussion and honourable dealing.

Any other way leads to bitterness at home and, in the larger sphere, war.

Manifesto [18]

Bertrand Russell and Albert Einstein

The manifesto was published in London over the joint names of these widely respected authorities on the 9th of July, 1955.

Though it went against the grain of public policy in the era of the cold war between the Soviet Union and the West, it tapped into a fear of nuclear warfare and further encouraged a widespread longing for peace and reconciliation.

In the tragic situation which confronts humanity, we feel that scientists should assemble in conference to appraise the perils that have arisen as a result of the development of weapons of mass destruction, and to discuss a resolution in the spirit of the appended draft.

We are speaking on this occasion, not as members of this or that nation, continent, or creed, but as human beings, members of the species Man, whose continued existence is in doubt. The world is full of conflicts; and, overshadowing all minor conflicts, the titanic struggle between Communism and anti-Communism.

Almost everybody who is politically conscious has strong feelings about one or more of these issues; but we want you, if you can, to set aside such feelings and consider yourselves only as members of a biological species which has had a remarkable history, and whose disappearance none of us can desire.

We shall try to say no single word which should appeal to one group rather than to another. All, equally, are in peril, and, if the peril is understood, there is hope that they may collectively avert it.

We have to learn to think in a new way. We have to learn to ask ourselves, not what steps can be taken to give military victory to whatever group we prefer, for there no longer are such steps; the question we have to ask ourselves is: what steps can be taken to prevent a military contest of which the issue must be disastrous to all parties?

The general public, and even many men in positions of authority, have not realized what would be involved in a war with nuclear bombs. The general public still thinks in terms of the obliteration of cities. It is understood that the new bombs are more powerful than the old, and that , while one A-bomb could obliterate Hiroshima, one H-bomb could obliterate the largest

---

[18] *https://pugwash.org/1955/07/09/statement-manifesto/#:~:text=In the tragic situation which,spirit of the appended draft.*

cities, such as London, New York, and Moscow.

No doubt in an H-bomb war, great cities would be obliterated. But this is one of the minor disasters that would have to be faced. If everybody in London, New York, and Moscow were exterminated, the world might, in the course of a few centuries, recover from the blow. But we now know, especially since the Bikini test, that nuclear bombs can gradually spread destruction over a very much wider area than had been supposed.

It is stated on very good authority that a bomb can now be manufactured which will be 2,500 times as powerful as that which destroyed Hiroshima. Such a bomb, if exploded near the ground or under water, sends radio-active particles into the upper air. They sink gradually and reach the surface of the earth in the form of a deadly dust or rain. It was this dust which infected the Japanese fishermen and their catch of fish. No one knows how widely such lethal radio-active particles might be diffused, but the best authorities are unanimous in saying that a war with H-bombs might possibly put an end to the human race. It is feared that if many H-bombs are used there will be universal death, sudden only for a minority, but for the majority a slow torture of disease and disintegration.

Many warnings have been uttered by eminent men of science and by authorities in military strategy. None of them will say that the worst results are certain. What they do say is that these results are possible, and no one can be sure that they will not be realized. We have not yet found that the views of experts on this question depend in any degree upon their politics or prejudices. They depend only, so far as our researches have revealed, upon the extent of the particular expert's knowledge. We have found that the men who know most are the most gloomy.

Here, then, is the problem which we present to you, stark and dreadful and inescapable: Shall we put an end to the human race; or shall mankind renounce war? People will not face this alternative because it is so difficult to abolish war.

The abolition of war will demand distasteful limitations of national sovereignty. But what perhaps impedes understanding of the situation more than anything else is that the term 'mankind' feels vague and abstract. People scarcely realize in imagination that the danger is to themselves and their children and their grandchildren, and not only to a dimly apprehended humanity. They can scarcely bring themselves to grasp that they, individually, and those whom they love are in imminent danger of perishing agonizingly. And so they hope that perhaps war may be allowed to continue provided modern weapons are prohibited.

This hope is illusory. Whatever agreements not to use H-bombs had been reached in time of peace, they would no longer be considered binding in time of war, and both sides would set to work to manufacture H-bombs as soon as war broke out, for, if one side manufactured the bombs and the other did not, the side that manufactured them would inevitably be victorious.

Although an agreement to renounce nuclear weapons as part of a general reduction of armaments would not afford an ultimate solution, it would serve certain important purposes. First, any agreement between East and West is to the good in so far as it tends to diminish tension. Second, the abolition of thermo-nuclear weapons, if each side believed that the other had carried it out sincerely, would lessen the fear of a sudden attack in the style of Pearl Harbour, which at present keeps both sides in a state of nervous apprehension. We should, therefore, welcome such an agreement though only as a first step.

Most of us are not neutral in feeling, but, as human beings, we have to remember that , if the issues between East and West are to be decided in any manner that can give any possible satisfaction to anybody, whether Communist or anti-Communist, whether Asian or European or American, whether White or Black, then these issues must not be decided by war. We should wish this to be understood, both in the East and in the West.

There lies before us, if we choose, continual progress in happiness, knowledge, and wisdom. Shall we, instead, choose death, because we cannot forget our quarrels? We appeal as human beings to human beings: Remember your humanity, and forget the rest. If you can do so, the way lies open to a new Paradise; if you cannot, there lies before you the risk of universal death.

Resolution:
WE invite this Congress, and through it the scientists of the world and the general public, to subscribe to the following resolution:

"In view of the fact that in any future world war nuclear weapons will certainly be employed, and that such weapons threaten the continued existence of mankind, we urge the governments of the world to realize, and to acknowledge publicly, that their purpose cannot be furthered by a world war, and we urge them, consequently, to find peaceful means for the settlement of all matters of dispute between them".

Pacem in terris—Peace on Earth [19]
Pope John XXIII

An encyclical of Pope John XXIII on establishing universal peace in truth, justice, charity, and liberty, issued on April 11, 1963. It was the first encyclical that a Pope had addressed not just to Catholics, but "to all men of good will".

Peace on Earth—which man throughout the ages has so longed for and sought after—can never be established, never guaranteed, except by the diligent observance of the divinely established order.

That a marvelous order predominates in the world of living beings and in the forces of nature, is the plain lesson which the progress of modern research and the discoveries of technology teach us. And it is part of the greatness of man that he can appreciate that order, and devise the means for harnessing those forces for his own benefit.

But what emerges first and foremost from the progress of scientific knowledge and the inventions of technology is the infinite greatness of God Himself, who created both man and the universe. Yes; out of nothing He made all things, and filled them with the fullness of His own wisdom and goodness. Hence, these are the words the holy psalmist used in praise of God: "O Lord, our Lord: how admirable is thy name in the whole earth!" And elsewhere he says: "How great are thy works, O Lord! Thou hast made all things in wisdom."

Moreover, God created man "in His own image and likeness," endowed him with intelligence and freedom, and made him lord of creation. All this the psalmist proclaims when he says: "Thou hast made him a little less than the angels: thou hast crowned him with glory and honour, and hast set him over the works of thy hands. Thou hast subjected all things under his feet."

And yet there is a disunity among individuals and among nations which is in striking contrast to this perfect order in the universe. One would think that the relationships that bind men together could only be governed by force.

But the world's Creator has stamped man's inmost being with an order revealed to man by his conscience; and his conscience insists on his preserving it. Men "show the work of the law written in their hearts. Their

---

[19] *https://www.vatican.va/content/john-xxiii/en/encyclicals/documents/hf_j-xxiii_enc_11041963_pacem.html/*

conscience bears witness to them". And how could it be otherwise? All created being reflects the infinite wisdom of God. It reflects it all the more clearly, the higher it stands in the scale of perfection.

Men's common interests make it imperative that at long last a world-wide community of nations be established.

We must devote our attention first of all to that order which should prevail among men

Any well-regulated and productive association of men in society demands the acceptance of one fundamental principle: that each individual man is truly a person. His is a nature that is endowed with intelligence and free will. As such, he has rights and duties, which together flow as a direct consequence from his nature. These rights and duties are universal and inviolable, and therefore altogether inalienable.

There is nothing human about a society that is welded together by force. Far from encouraging, as it should, the attainment of man's progress and perfection, it is merely an obstacle to his freedom.

God has created men social by nature, and a society cannot "hold together unless someone is in command to give effective direction and unity of purpose. Hence every civilized community must have a ruling authority, and this authority, no less than society itself, has its source in nature, and consequently has God for its author".

But it must not be imagined that authority knows no bounds. Since its starting point is the permission to govern in accordance with right reason, there is no escaping the conclusion that it derives its binding force from the moral order, which in turn has God as its origin and end.

Hence, a regime which governs solely or mainly by means of threats and intimidation or promises of reward, provides men with no effective incentive to work for the common good. And even if it did, it would certainly be offensive to the dignity of free and rational human beings. Authority is before all else a moral force. For this reason the appeal of rulers should be to the individual conscience, to the duty which every man has of voluntarily contributing to the common good. But since all men are equal in natural dignity, no man has the capacity to force internal compliance on another. Only God can do that, for He alone scrutinizes and judges the secret counsels of the heart.

But one of the principal imperatives of the common good is the recognition of the moral order and the unfailing observance of its precepts. "A firmly established order between political communities must be founded on the unshakable and unmoving rock of the moral law, that law which is revealed in the order of nature by the Creator Himself, and engraved indelibly on men's hearts... Its principles are beacon lights to guide the policies of men and nations. They are also warning lights—providential signs—which men must heed if their laborious efforts to establish a new order are not to encounter perilous storms and shipwreck".

Relations between States must be regulated by justice. This necessitates both the recognition of their mutual rights, and, at the same time, the fulfilment of their respective duties.

States have the right to existence, to self development, and to the means necessary to achieve this. They have the right to play the leading part in the process of their own development, and the right to their good name and due honours. Consequently, States are likewise in duty bound to safeguard all such rights effectively, and to avoid any action that could violate them. And just as individual men may not pursue their own private interests in a way that is unfair and detrimental to others, so too it would be criminal in a State to aim at improving itself by the use of methods which involve other nations in injury and unjust oppression. There is a saying of St. Augustine which has particular relevance in this context: "Take away justice, and what are kingdoms but mighty bands of robbers".

There may be, and sometimes is, a clash of interests among States, each striving for its own development. When differences of this sort arise, they must be settled in a truly human way, not by armed force, nor by deceit or trickery. There must be a mutual assessment of the arguments and feelings on both sides, a mature and objective investigation of the situation, and an equitable reconciliation of opposing views.

Since relationships between States must be regulated in accordance with the principles of truth and justice, States must further these relationships by taking positive steps to pool their material and spiritual resources. In many cases this can be achieved by all kinds of mutual collaboration; and this is already happening in our own day in the economic, social, political, educational, health and athletic spheres—and with beneficial results. We must bear in mind that of its very nature civil authority exists, not to confine men within the frontiers of their own nations, but primarily to protect the common good of the State, which certainly cannot be divorced from the common good of the entire human family.

Thus, in pursuing their own interests, civil societies, far from causing injury to others, must join plans and forces whenever the efforts of particular States cannot achieve the desired goal. But in doing so great care must be taken. What is beneficial to some States may prove detrimental rather than advantageous to others.

We are deeply distressed to see the enormous stocks of armaments that have been, and continue to be, manufactured in the economically more developed countries. This policy is involving a vast outlay of intellectual and material resources, with the result that the people of these countries are saddled with a great burden, while other countries lack the help they need for their economic and social development.

There is a common belief that under modern conditions peace cannot be assured except on the basis of an equal balance of armaments and that this factor is the probable cause of this stockpiling of armaments. Thus, if one country increases its military strength, others are immediately roused by a competitive spirit to augment their own supply of armaments. And if one country is equipped with atomic weapons, others consider themselves justified in producing such weapons themselves, equal in destructive force.

Consequently people are living in the grip of constant fear. They are afraid that at any moment the impending storm may break upon them with horrific violence. And they have good reasons for their fear, for there is certainly no lack of such weapons. While it is difficult to believe that anyone would dare to assume responsibility for initiating the appalling slaughter and destruction that war would bring in its wake, there is no denying that the conflagration could be started by some chance and unforeseen circumstance. Moreover, even though the monstrous power of modern weapons does indeed act as a deterrent, there is reason to fear that the very testing of nuclear devices for war purposes can, if continued, lead to serious danger for various forms of life on earth.

Hence justice, right reason, and the recognition of man's dignity cry out insistently for a cessation to the arms race. The stock-piles of armaments which have been built up in various countries must be reduced all round and simultaneously by the parties concerned. Nuclear weapons must be banned. A general agreement must be reached on a suitable disarmament program, with an effective system of mutual control. In the words of Pope Pius XII: "The calamity of a world war, with the economic and social ruin and the moral excesses and dissolution that accompany it, must not on any account be permitted to engulf the human race for a third time".

Everyone, however, must realize that, unless this process of disarmament be thoroughgoing and complete, and reach men's very souls, it is impossible to stop the arms race, or to reduce armaments, or—and this is the main thing—ultimately to abolish them entirely. Everyone must sincerely co-operate in the effort to banish fear and the anxious expectation of war from men's minds. But this requires that the fundamental principles upon which peace is based in today's world be replaced by an altogether different one, namely, the realization that true and lasting peace among nations cannot consist in the possession of an equal supply of armaments but only in mutual trust. And We are confident that this can be achieved, for it is a thing which not only is dictated by common sense, but is in itself most desirable and most fruitful of good.

Here, then, we have an objective dictated first of all by reason. There is general agreement—or at least there should be—that relations between States, as between individuals, must be regulated not by armed force, but in accordance with the principles of right reason: the principles, that is, of truth, justice and vigorous and sincere co-operation.

Secondly, it is an objective which we maintain is more earnestly to be desired. For who is there who does not feel the craving to be rid of the threat of war, and to see peace preserved and made daily more secure?

And finally it is an objective which is rich with possibilities for good. Its advantages will be felt everywhere, by individuals, by families, by nations, by the whole human race. The warning of Pope Pius XII still rings in our ears: "Nothing is lost by peace; everything may be lost by war."u

We therefore consider it our duty as the vicar on earth of Jesus Christ—the Saviour of the world, the Author of peace—and as interpreter of the most ardent wishes of the whole human family, in the fatherly love We bear all mankind, to beg and beseech mankind, and above all the rulers of States, to be unsparing of their labour and efforts to ensure that human affairs follow a rational and dignified course.

In their deliberations together, let men of outstanding wisdom and influence give serious thought to the problem of achieving a more human adjustment of relations between States throughout the world. It must be an adjustment that is based on mutual trust, sincerity in negotiation, and the faithful fulfilment of obligations assumed. Every aspect of the problem must be examined, so that eventually there may emerge some point of agreement from which to initiate treaties which are sincere, lasting, and beneficial in their effects.

We, for our part, will pray unceasingly that God may bless these labours by His divine assistance, and make them fruitful.

Furthermore, relations between States must be regulated by the principle of freedom. This means that no country has the right to take any action that would constitute an unjust oppression of other countries, or an unwarranted interference in their affairs. On the contrary, all should help to develop in others an increasing awareness of their duties, an adventurous and enterprising spirit, and the resolution to take the initiative for their own advancement in every field of endeavour.

Men nowadays are becoming more and more convinced that any disputes which may arise between nations must be resolved by negotiation and agreement, and not by recourse to arms.

We acknowledge that this conviction owes its origin chiefly to the terrifying destructive force of modern weapons. It arises from fear of the ghastly and catastrophic consequences of their use. Thus, in this age which boasts of its atomic power, it no longer makes sense to maintain that war is a fit instrument with which to repair the violation of justice.

And yet, unhappily, we often find the law of fear reigning supreme among nations and causing them to spend enormous sums on armaments. Their object is not aggression, so they say—and there is no reason for disbelieving them—but to deter others from aggression.

Nevertheless, We are hopeful that, by establishing contact with one another and by a policy of negotiation, nations will come to a better recognition of the natural ties that bind them together as men. We are hopeful, too, that they will come to a fairer realization of one of the cardinal duties deriving from our common nature: namely, that love, not fear, must dominate the relationships between individuals and between nations. It is principally characteristic of love that it draws men together in all sorts of ways, sincerely united in the bonds of mind and matter; and this is a union from which countless blessings can flow.

Hence among the very serious obligations incumbent upon men of high principles, We must include the task of establishing new relationships in human society, under the mastery and guidance of truth, justice, charity and freedom—relations between individual citizens, between citizens and their respective States, between States, and finally between individuals, families, intermediate associations and States on the one hand, and the world community on the other. There is surely no one who will not consider this a most exalted task, for it is one which is able to bring about true peace in accordance with divinely established order.

Considering the need, the men who are shouldering this responsibility are far too few in number, yet they are deserving of the highest recognition from society, and We rightfully honour them with Our public praise. We call upon them to persevere in their ideals, which are of such tremendous benefit to mankind. At the same time We are encouraged to hope that many more men, Christians especially, will join their cause, spurred on by love and the realization of their duty. Everyone who has joined the ranks of Christ must be a glowing point of light in the world, a nucleus of love, a leaven of the whole mass. He will be so in proportion to his degree of spiritual union with God.

The world will never be the dwelling place of peace, till peace has found a home in the heart of each and every man, till every man preserves in himself the order ordained by God to be preserved. That is why St.

Augustine asks the question: "Does your mind desire the strength to gain the mastery over your passions? Let it submit to a greater power, and it will conquer all beneath it. And peace will be in you—true, sure, most ordered peace. What is that order? God as ruler of the mind; the mind as ruler of the body. Nothing could be more orderly".

Our concern here has been with problems which are causing men extreme anxiety at the present time; problems which are intimately bound up with the progress of human society. Unquestionably, the teaching We have given has been inspired by a longing which We feel most keenly, and which We know is shared by all men of good will: that peace may be assured on earth.

We who, in spite of Our inadequacy, are nevertheless the vicar of Him whom the prophet announced as the Prince of Peace, conceive of it as Our duty to devote all Our thoughts and care and energy to further this common good of all mankind. Yet peace is but an empty word, if it does not rest upon that order which Our hope prevailed upon Us to set forth in outline in this encyclical. It is an order that is founded on truth, built up on justice, nurtured and animated by charity, and brought into effect under the auspices of freedom.

So magnificent, so exalted is this aim that human resources alone, even though inspired by the most praiseworthy good will, cannot hope to achieve it. God Himself must come to man's aid with His heavenly assistance, if human society is to bear the closest possible resemblance to the kingdom of God.

Let us, then, pray with all fervour for this peace which our divine Redeemer came to bring us. May He banish from the souls of men whatever might endanger peace. May He transform all men into witnesses of truth, justice and brotherly love. May He illumine with His light the minds of rulers, so that, besides caring for the proper material welfare of their peoples, they may also guarantee them the fairest gift of peace.

Finally, may Christ inflame the desires of all men to break through the barriers which divide them, to strengthen the bonds of mutual love, to learn to understand one another, and to pardon those who have done them wrong. Through His power and inspiration may all peoples welcome each other to their hearts as brothers, and may the peace they long for ever flower and ever reign among them.

The quest for peace and justice [20]
Martin Luther King

This is the address by the Baptist minister Martin Luther King on receiving the Nobel Peace Prize in 1964. Through his activist leadership of the 1950s-60s American Civil Rights Movement he became one of the most effective and charismatic, yet humble, workers for peace and justice, both racial and other, in America and, as a consequence, world-wide.

He paid the price for his beliefs, assassinated in 1968, but long remembered for the impact of his vision, actions and, in even the most difficult conditions, commitment to non-violence.

Occasionally in life there are those moments of unutterable fulfilment which cannot be completely explained by those symbols called words. Their meaning can only be articulated by the inaudible language of the heart. Such is the moment I am presently experiencing. I experience this high and joyous moment not for myself alone but for those devotees of nonviolence who have moved so courageously against the ramparts of racial injustice and who in the process have acquired a new estimate of their own human worth. Many of them are young and cultured. Others are middle aged and middle class. The majority are poor and untutored. But they are all united in the quiet conviction that it is better to suffer in dignity than to accept segregation in humiliation. These are the real heroes of the freedom struggle: they are the noble people for whom I accept the Nobel Peace Prize.

This evening I would like to use this lofty and historic platform to discuss what appears to me to be the most pressing problem confronting mankind today. Modern man has brought this whole world to an awe-inspiring threshold of the future. He has reached new and astonishing peaks of scientific success. He has produced machines that think and instruments that peer into the unfathomable ranges of interstellar space. He has built gigantic bridges to span the seas and gargantuan buildings to kiss the skies. His airplanes and spaceships have dwarfed distance, placed time in chains, and carved highways through the stratosphere. This is a dazzling picture of modern man's scientific and technological progress.

Yet, in spite of these spectacular strides in science and technology, and still unlimited ones to come, something basic is missing. There is a sort of poverty of the spirit which stands in glaring contrast to our scientific and technological abundance. The richer we have become materially, the

---

[20] *https://www.nobelprize.org/prizes/peace/1964/king/lecture/ excerpts quoted by permission.*

poorer we have become morally and spiritually. We have learned to fly the air like birds and swim the sea like fish, but we have not learned the simple art of living together as brothers.

Every man lives in two realms, the internal and the external. The internal is that realm of spiritual ends expressed in art, literature, morals, and religion. The external is that complex of devices, techniques, mechanisms, and instrumentalities by means of which we live. Our problem today is that we have allowed the internal to become lost in the external. We have allowed the means by which we live to outdistance the ends for which we live. So much of modern life can be summarized in that arresting dictum of the poet Thoreau[1]: "Improved means to an unimproved end". This is the serious predicament, the deep and haunting problem confronting modern man. If we are to survive today, our moral and spiritual "lag" must be eliminated. Enlarged material powers spell enlarged peril if there is not proportionate growth of the soul. When the "without" of man's nature subjugates the "within", dark storm clouds begin to form in the world.

This problem of spiritual and moral lag, which constitutes modern man's chief dilemma, expresses itself in three larger problems which grow out of man's ethical infantilism. Each of these problems, while appearing to be separate and isolated, is inextricably bound to the other. I refer to racial injustice, poverty, and war.

The first problem that I would like to mention is racial injustice. The struggle to eliminate the evil of racial injustice constitutes one of the major struggles of our time. The present upsurge of the Negro people of the United States grows out of a deep and passionate determination to make freedom and equality a reality "here" and "now". In one sense the civil rights movement in the United States is a special American phenomenon which must be understood in the light of American history and dealt with in terms of the American situation. But on another and more important level, what is happening in the United States today is a relatively small part of a world development.

We live in a day, says the philosopher Alfred North Whitehead[2],"when civilization is shifting its basic outlook: a major turning point in history where the presuppositions on which society is structured are being analyzed, sharply challenged, and profoundly changed." What we are seeing now is a freedom explosion, the realization of "an idea whose time has come", to use Victor Hugo's phrase. The deep rumbling of discontent that we hear today is the thunder of disinherited masses, rising from dungeons of oppression to the bright hills of freedom, in one majestic chorus the rising masses singing, in the words of our freedom song, "Ain't gonna let nobody turn us around."[4] All over the world, like a fever, the freedom movement is spreading in the widest liberation in history. The great masses of people are determined to end the exploitation of their races and land. They are awake and moving toward their goal like a tidal wave. You can hear them rumbling in every village street, on the docks, in the houses, among the students, in the churches, and at political meetings. Historic movement was for several centuries that of the nations and societies of Western Europe out into the rest of the world in "conquest" of various sorts. That period, the era of colonialism, is at an end. East is meeting West. The earth is being redistributed. Yes, we are "shifting our basic outlooks".

These developments should not surprise any student of history. Oppressed people cannot remain oppressed forever. The yearning for freedom eventually manifests itself. The Bible tells the thrilling story of how Moses stood in Pharaoh's court centuries ago and cried, "Let my people go." This is a kind of opening chapter in a continuing story. The present struggle in the United States is a later chapter in the same unfolding story. Something within has reminded the Negro of his birthright of freedom, and something without has reminded him that it can be gained. Consciously or unconsciously, he has been caught up by the *Zeitgeist*, and with his black brothers of Africa and his brown and yellow brothers in Asia, South America, and the Caribbean, the United States Negro is moving with a sense of great urgency toward the promised land of racial justice.

Fortunately, some significant strides have been made in the struggle to end the long night of racial injustice. We have seen the magnificent drama of independence unfold in Asia and Africa. Just thirty years ago there were only three independent nations in the whole of Africa. But today thirty-five African nations have risen from colonial bondage. In the United States we have witnessed the gradual demise of the system of racial segregation. The Supreme Court's decision of 1954 outlawing segregation in the public schools gave a legal and constitutional deathblow to the whole doctrine of separate but equal6. The Court decreed that separate facilities are inherently unequal and that to segregate a child on the basis of race is to deny that child equal protection of the law. This decision came as a beacon light of hope to millions of disinherited people. Then came that glowing day a few months ago when a strong Civil Rights Bill became the law of our land. This bill, which was first recommended and promoted by President Kennedy, was passed because of the overwhelming support and perseverance of millions of Americans, Negro and white. It came as a bright interlude in the long and sometimes turbulent struggle for civil rights: the beginning of a second emancipation proclamation providing a comprehensive legal basis for equality of opportunity. Since the passage of this bill we have seen some encouraging and surprising signs of compliance. I am happy to report that, by and large, communities all over the southern part of the United States are obeying the Civil Rights Law and showing remarkable good sense in the process.

Another indication that progress is being made was found in the recent presidential election in the United States. The American people revealed great maturity by overwhelmingly rejecting a presidential candidate who had become identified with extremism, racism, and retrogression8. The voters of our nation rendered a telling blow to the radical right. They defeated those elements in our society which seek to pit white against Negro and lead the nation down a dangerous Fascist path.

Let me not leave you with a false impression. The problem is far from solved. We still have a long, long way to go before the dream of freedom is a reality for the Negro in the United States. To put it figuratively in biblical language, we have left the dusty soils of Egypt and crossed a Red Sea whose waters had for years been hardened by a long and piercing winter of massive resistance. But before we reach the majestic shores of the Promised Land, there is a frustrating and bewildering wilderness ahead. We must still face prodigious hilltops of opposition and gigantic mountains of resistance. But with patient and firm determination we will press on until every valley of despair is exalted to new peaks of hope, until every mountain of pride and irrationality is made low by the leveling process of humility and compassion; until the rough places of injustice are transformed into a smooth plane of equality of opportunity; and until the crooked places of prejudice are transformed by the straightening process of bright-eyed wisdom.

What the main sections of the civil rights movement in the United States are saying is that the demand for dignity, equality, jobs, and citizenship will not be abandoned or diluted or postponed. If that means resistance and conflict we shall not flinch. We shall not be cowed. We are no longer afraid.

The word that symbolizes the spirit and the outward form of our encounter is *nonviolence*, and it is doubtless that factor which made it seem appropriate to award a peace prize to one identified with struggle. Broadly speaking, nonviolence in the civil rights struggle has meant not relying on arms and weapons of struggle. It has meant noncooperation with customs and laws which are institutional aspects of a regime of discrimination and enslavement. It has meant direct participation of masses in protest, rather than reliance on indirect methods which frequently do not involve masses in action at all.

Nonviolence has also meant that my people in the agonizing struggles of recent years have taken suffering upon themselves instead of inflicting it on others. It has meant, as I said, that we are no longer afraid and cowed. But in some substantial degree it has meant that we do not want to instill fear in others or into the society of which we are a part. The movement does not seek to liberate Negroes at the expense of the humiliation and enslavement of whites. It seeks no victory over anyone. It seeks to liberate American society and to share in the self-liberation of all the people.

Violence as a way of achieving racial justice is both impractical and immoral. I am not unmindful of the fact that violence often brings about momentary results. Nations have frequently won their independence in battle. But in spite of temporary victories, violence never brings permanent peace. It solves no social problem: it merely creates new and more complicated ones. Violence is impractical because it is a descending spiral ending in destruction for all. It is immoral because it seeks to humiliate the opponent rather than win his understanding: it seeks to annihilate rather than convert. Violence is immoral because it thrives on hatred rather than love. It destroys community and makes brotherhood impossible. It leaves society in monologue rather than dialogue. Violence ends up defeating itself. It creates bitterness in the survivors and brutality in the destroyers.

In a real sense nonviolence seeks to redeem the spiritual and moral lag that I spoke of earlier as the chief dilemma of modern man. It seeks to secure moral ends through moral means. Nonviolence is a powerful and just weapon. Indeed, it is a weapon unique in history, which cuts without wounding and ennobles the man who wields it.

I believe in this method because I think it is the only way to reestablish a broken community. It is the method which seeks to implement the just law by appealing to the conscience of the great decent majority who through blindness, fear, pride, and irrationality have allowed their consciences to sleep.

The nonviolent resisters can summarize their message in the following simple terms: we will take direct action against injustice despite the failure of governmental and other official agencies to act first. We will not obey unjust laws or submit to unjust practices. We will do this peacefully, openly, cheerfully because our aim is to persuade. We adopt the means of nonviolence because our end is a community at peace with itself. We will try to persuade with our words, but if our words fail, we will try to persuade with our acts. We will always be willing to talk and seek fair compromise, but we are ready to suffer when necessary and even risk our lives to become witnesses to truth as we see it.

This approach to the problem of racial injustice is not at all without successful precedent. It was used in a magnificent way by Mohandas K. Gandhi to challenge the might of the British Empire and free his people from the political domination and economic exploitation inflicted upon them for centuries. He struggled only with the weapons of truth, soul force, non-injury, and courage.

In the past ten years unarmed gallant men and women of the United States have given living testimony to the moral power and efficacy of nonviolence. By the thousands, faceless, anonymous, relentless young people, black and white, have temporarily left the ivory towers of learning for the barricades of bias. Their courageous and disciplined activities have come as a refreshing oasis in a desert sweltering with the heat of injustice. They have taken our whole nation back to those great wells of democracy which were dug deep by the founding fathers in the formulation of the Constitution and the Declaration of Independence. One day all of America will be proud of their achievements.

I am only too well aware of the human weaknesses and failures which exist, the doubts about the efficacy of nonviolence, and the open advocacy of violence by some. But I am still convinced that nonviolence is both the most practically sound and morally excellent way to grapple with the age-old problem of racial injustice.

A second evil which plagues the modern world is that of poverty. Like a monstrous octopus, it projects its nagging, prehensile tentacles in lands and villages all over the world. Almost two-thirds of the peoples of the world go to bed hungry at night. They are undernourished, ill-housed, and shabbily clad. Many of them have no houses or beds to sleep in. Their only beds are the sidewalks of the cities and the dusty roads of the villages. Most of these poverty-stricken children of God have never seen a physician or a dentist. This problem of poverty is not only seen in the class division between the highly developed industrial nations and the so-called underdeveloped nations; it is seen in the great economic gaps within the rich nations themselves. Take my own country for example. We have developed the greatest system of production that history has ever known. We have become the richest nation in the world. Our national gross product this year will reach the astounding figure of almost 650 billion dollars.

Yet, at least one-fifth of our fellow citizens - some ten million families, comprising about forty million individuals - are bound to a miserable culture of poverty. In a sense the poverty of the poor in America is more frustrating than the poverty of Africa and Asia. The misery of the poor in Africa and Asia is shared misery, a fact of life for the vast majority; they are all poor together as a result of years of exploitation and underdevelopment. In sad contrast, the poor in America know that they live in the richest nation in the world, and that even though they are perishing on a lonely island of poverty they are surrounded by a vast ocean of material prosperity. Glistening towers of glass and steel easily seen from their slum dwellings spring up almost overnight. Jet liners speed over their ghettoes at 600 miles an hour; satellites streak through outer space and reveal details of the moon. President Johnson, in his

State of the Union Message, emphasized this contradiction when he heralded the United States' "highest standard of living in the world", and deplored that it was accompanied by "dislocation; loss of jobs, and the specter of poverty in the midst of plenty".

So it is obvious that if man is to redeem his spiritual and moral "lag", he must go all out to bridge the social and economic gulf between the "haves" and the "have nots" of the world. Poverty is one of the most urgent items on the agenda of modern life.

There is nothing new about poverty. What is new, however, is that we have the resources to get rid of it. More than a century and a half ago people began to be disturbed about the twin problems of population and production. A thoughtful Englishman named Malthus wrote a book that set forth some rather frightening conclusions. He predicted that the human family was gradually moving toward global starvation because the world was producing people faster than it was producing food and material to support them. Later scientists, however, disproved the conclusion of Malthus, and revealed that he had vastly underestimated the resources of the world and the resourcefulness of man.

Not too many years ago, Dr. Kirtley Mather, a Harvard geologist, wrote a book entitled *Enough and to Spare*. He set forth the basic theme that famine is wholly unnecessary in the modern world. Today, therefore, the question on the agenda must read: Why should there be hunger and privation in any land, in any city, at any table when man has the resources and the scientific know-how to provide all mankind with the basic necessities of life? Even deserts can be irrigated and top soil can be replaced. We cannot complain of a lack of land, for there are twenty-five million square miles of tillable land, of which we are using less than seven million. We have amazing knowledge of vitamins, nutrition, the chemistry of food, and the versatility of atoms. There is no deficit in human resources; the deficit is in human will. The well-off and the secure have too often become indifferent and oblivious to the poverty and deprivation in their midst. The poor in our countries have been shut out of our minds, and driven from the mainstream of our societies, because we have allowed them to become invisible. Just as nonviolence exposed the ugliness of racial injustice, so must the infection and sickness of poverty be exposed and healed - not only its symptoms but its basic causes. This, too, will be a fierce struggle, but we must not be afraid to pursue the remedy no matter how formidable the task.

The time has come for an all-out world war against poverty. The rich nations must use their vast resources of wealth to develop the underdeveloped, school the unschooled, and feed the unfed. Ultimately a great nation is a compassionate nation. No individual or nation can be great if it does not have a concern for "the least of these". Deeply etched in the fiber of our religious tradition is the conviction that men are made in the image of God and that they are souls of infinite metaphysical value, the heirs of a legacy of dignity and worth. If we feel this as a profound moral fact, we cannot be content to see men hungry, to see men victimized with starvation and ill health when we have the means to help them. The wealthy nations must go all out to bridge the gulf between the rich minority and the poor majority.

In the final analysis, the rich must not ignore the poor because both rich and poor are tied in a single garment of destiny. All life is interrelated, and all men are interdependent. The agony of the poor diminishes the rich, and the salvation of the poor enlarges the rich. We are inevitably our brothers' keeper because of the interrelated structure of reality. John Donne interpreted this truth in graphic terms when he affirmed:

"No man is an Iland, intire of its selfe:
every man is a peece of the Continent,
a part of the maine:
if a Clod bee washed away by the Sea,
Europe is the lesse,
as well as if a Promontorie were,
as well as if a Mannor of thy friends
or of thine owne were:
any mans death diminishes me,
because I am involved in Mankinde:
and therefore never send to know
for whom the bell tolls: it tolls for thee."

A third great evil confronting our world is that of war. Recent events have vividly reminded us that nations are not reducing but rather increasing their arsenals of weapons of mass destruction. The best brains in the highly developed nations of the world are devoted to military technology. The proliferation of nuclear weapons has not been halted, in spite of the Limited Test Ban Treaty16. On the contrary, the detonation of an atomic device by the first nonwhite, non- Western, and so-called underdeveloped power, namely the Chinese People's Republic17, opens new vistas of exposure of vast multitudes, the whole of humanity, to insidious terrorization by the ever-present threat of annihilation. The fact that most of the time human beings put the truth about the nature and risks of the nuclear war out of their minds because it is too painful and therefore not "acceptable", does not alter the nature and risks of such war. The device of "rejection" may temporarily cover up anxiety, but it does not bestow peace of mind and emotional security.

So man's proneness to engage in war is still a fact. But wisdom born of experience should tell us that war is obsolete. There may have been a time when war served as a negative good by preventing the spread and growth of an evil force, but the destructive power of modern weapons eliminated even the possibility that war may serve as a negative good. If we assume that life is worth living and that man has a right to survive, then we must find an alternative to war. In a day when vehicles hurtle through outer space and guided ballistic missiles carve highways of death through the stratosphere, no nation can claim victory in war. A so-called limited war will leave little more than a calamitous legacy of human suffering, political turmoil, and spiritual disillusionment. A world war - God forbid! - will leave only smoldering ashes as a mute testimony of a human race whose folly led inexorably to ultimate death. So if modern man continues to flirt unhesitatingly with war, he will transform his earthly habitat into an inferno such as even the mind of Dante could not imagine.

Therefore, I venture to suggest to all of you and all who hear and may eventually read these words, that the philosophy and strategy of nonviolence become immediately a subject for study and for serious experimentation in every field of human conflict, by no means excluding the relations between nations. It is, after all, nation-states which make war, which have produced the weapons which threaten the survival of mankind, and which are both genocidal and suicidal in character.

Here also we have ancient habits to deal with, vast structures of power, indescribably complicated problems to solve. But unless we abdicate our humanity altogether and succumb to fear and impotence in the presence of the weapons we have ourselves created, it is as imperative and urgent to put an end to war and violence between nations as it is to put an end to racial injustice. Equality with whites will hardly solve the problems of either whites or Negroes if it means equality in a society under the spell of terror and a world doomed to extinction.

I do not wish to minimize the complexity of the problems that need to be faced in achieving disarmament and peace. But I think it is a fact that we shall not have the will, the courage, and the insight to deal with such matters unless in this field we are prepared to undergo a mental and spiritual reevaluation - a change of focus which will enable us to see that the things which seem most real and powerful are indeed now unreal and have come under the sentence of death. We need to make a supreme effort to generate the readiness, indeed the eagerness, to enter into the new world which is now possible, "the city which hath foundations, whose builder and maker is God".

We will not build a peaceful world by following a negative path. It is not enough to say "We must not wage war." It is necessary to love peace and sacrifice for it. We must concentrate not merely on the negative expulsion of war, but on the positive affirmation of peace. There is a fascinating little story that is preserved for us in Greek literature about Ulysses and the Sirens. The Sirens had the ability to sing so sweetly that sailors could not resist steering toward their island. Many ships were lured upon the rocks, and men forgot home, duty, and honor as they flung themselves into the sea to be embraced by arms that drew them down to death. Ulysses, determined not to be lured by the Sirens, first decided to tie himself tightly to the mast of his boat, and his crew stuffed their ears with wax. But finally he and his crew learned a better way to save themselves: they took on board the beautiful singer Orpheus whose melodies were sweeter than the music of the Sirens. When Orpheus sang, who bothered to listen to the Sirens?

So we must fix our vision not merely on the negative expulsion of war, but upon the positive affirmation of peace. We must see that peace represents a sweeter music, a cosmic melody that is far superior to the discords of war. Somehow we must transform the dynamics of the world power struggle from the negative nuclear arms race which no one can win to a positive contest to harness man's creative genius for the purpose of making peace and prosperity a reality for all of the nations of the world. In short, we must shift the arms race into a "peace race". If we have the will and determination to mount such a peace offensive, we will unlock hitherto tightly sealed doors of hope and transform our imminent cosmic elegy into a psalm of creative fulfillment.

All that I have said boils down to the point of affirming that mankind's survival is dependent upon man's ability to solve the problems of racial injustice, poverty, and war; the solution of these problems is in turn dependent upon man squaring his moral progress with his scientific progress, and learning the practical art of living in harmony. Some years ago a famous novelist died. Among his papers was found a list of suggested story plots for future stories, the most prominently underscored being this one: "A widely separated family inherits a house in which they have to live together." This is the great new problem of mankind. We have inherited a big house, a great "world house" in which we have to live together - black and white, Easterners and Westerners, Gentiles and Jews, Catholics and Protestants, Moslem and Hindu, a family unduly separated in ideas, culture, and interests who, because we can never again live without each other, must learn, somehow, in this one big world, to live with each other.

This means that more and more our loyalties must become ecumenical rather than sectional. We must now give an overriding loyalty to mankind as a whole in order to preserve the best in our individual societies.

This call for a worldwide fellowship that lifts neighbourly concern beyond one's tribe, race, class, and nation is in reality a call for an all-embracing and unconditional love for all men. This oft misunderstood and misinterpreted concept so readily dismissed by the Nietzsches of the world as a weak and cowardly force, has now become an absolute necessity for the survival of man. When I speak of love I am not speaking of some sentimental and weak response which is little more than emotional bosh. I am speaking of that force which all of the great religions have seen as the supreme unifying principle of life. Love is somehow the key that unlocks the door which leads to ultimate reality. This Hindu-Moslem-Christian-Jewish-Buddhist belief about ultimate reality is beautifully summed up in the First Epistle of Saint John:

"Let us love one another: for love is of God; and everyone
that loveth is born of God, and knoweth God.
He that loveth not knoweth not God; for God is love.
If we love one another, God dwelleth in us, and His
love is perfected in us."

Let us hope that this spirit will become the order of the day. As Arnold Toynbee20 says: "Love is the ultimate force that makes for the saving choice of life and good against the damning choice of death and evil. Therefore the first hope in our inventory must be the hope that love is going to have the last word." We can no longer afford to worship the God of hate or bow before the altar of retaliation. The oceans of history are made turbulent by the ever-rising tides of hate. History is cluttered with the wreckage of nations and individuals that pursued this self-defeating path of hate. Love is the key to the solution of the problems of the world.

Let me close by saying that I have the personal faith that mankind will somehow rise up to the occasion and give new directions to an age drifting rapidly to its doom. In spite of the tensions and uncertainties of this period something profoundly meaningful is taking place. Old systems of exploitation and oppression are passing away, and out of the womb of a frail world new systems of justice and equality are being born. Doors of opportunity are gradually being opened to those at the bottom of society. The shirtless and barefoot people of the land are developing a new sense of "some-bodiness" and carving a tunnel of hope through the dark mountain of despair. "The people who sat in darkness have seen a great light." Here and there an individual or group dares to love, and rises to the majestic heights of moral maturity. So in a real sense this is a great time to be alive. Therefore, I am not yet discouraged about the future. Granted that the easygoing optimism of yesterday is impossible.

Granted that those who pioneer in the struggle for peace and freedom will still face uncomfortable jail terms, painful threats of death; they will still be battered by the storms of persecution, leading them to the nagging feeling that they can no longer bear such a heavy burden, and the temptation of wanting to retreat to a more quiet and serene life. Granted that we face a world crisis which leaves us standing so often amid the surging murmur of life's restless sea. But every crisis has both its dangers and its opportunities. It can spell either salvation or doom. In a dark confused world the kingdom of God may yet reign in the hearts of men.

The beginning of peace is love [21]
Mother Teresa

Mother Teresa (1910–1997) was born in Macedonia, and joined the Sisters of Loreto in Dublin in 1928. She left the order in 1948 to set up the Missionaries of Charity in Calcutta, dedicated to serving the poorest of the poor. This became her life's work. She was awarded the Nobel Peace Prize in 1979 and beatified in 2003.

From the slums of Calcutta, her writings and sayings have rung round the world and contributed mightily to the search for peace—for individuals, for the world—such as:

> *"Kind words can be short and easy to speak, but their echoes are truly endless".*

> *"Every time you smile at someone, it is an action of love, a gift to that person, a beautiful thing".*

> *"Not all of us can do great things. But we can do small things with great love".*

As we have gathered here together to thank God for the Nobel Peace Prize I think it will be beautiful that we pray the prayer of St. Francis of Assisi which always surprises me very much—we pray this prayer every day after Holy Communion, because it is very fitting for each one of us, and I always wonder that 4-500 years ago as St. Francis of Assisi composed this prayer that they had the same difficulties that we have today, as we compose this prayer that fits very nicely for us also. I think some of you already have got it—so we will pray together

'Lord, make me an instrument of your peace
Where there is hatred, let me sow love
Where there is injury, pardon
Where there is doubt, faith… '

Let us thank God for the opportunity that we all have together today, for this gift of peace that reminds us that we have been created to live that peace, and Jesus became man to bring that good news to the poor. He being God became man in all things like us except sin, and he proclaimed very clearly that he had come to give the good news. The news was peace to all of good will and this is something that we all want—the peace of heart—and God loved the world so much that he gave his son—it was

---

[21] https://outlook.office365.com/owa/?realm=open.ac.uk/ *excerpts quoted by permission.*

a giving—it is as much as if to say it hurt God to give, because he loved the world so much that he gave his son, and he gave him to Virgin Mary, and what did she do with him?

As soon as he came in her life—immediately she went in haste to give that good news, and as she came into the house of her cousin, the child—the unborn child—the child in the womb of Elizabeth, leapt with joy. He was that little unborn child, was the first messenger of peace. He recognised the Prince of Peace, he recognised that Christ has come to bring the good news for you and for me. And as if that was not enough—it was not enough to become a man—he died on the cross to show that greater love, and he died for you and for me and for that leper and for that man dying of hunger and that naked person lying in the street not only of Calcutta, but of Africa, and New York, and London, and Oslo—and insisted that we love one another as he loves each one of us. And we read that in the Gospel very clearly—love as I have loved you—as I love you—as the Father has loved me, I love you—and the harder the Father loved him, he gave him to us, and how much we love one another, we, too, must give each other until it hurts. It is not enough for us to say: I love God, but I do not love my neighbour. St. John says you are a liar if you say you love God and you don't love your neighbour. How can you love God whom you do not see, if you do not love your neighbour whom you see, whom you touch, with whom you live.

And so this is very important for us to realise that love, to be true, has to hurt. It hurt Jesus to love us, it hurt him. And to make sure we remember his great love he made himself the bread of life to satisfy our hunger for his love. Our hunger for God, because we have been created for that love. We have been created in his image. We have been created to love and be loved, and then he has become man to make it possible for us to love as he loved us. He makes himself the hungry one—the naked one—the homeless one—the sick one—the one in prison—the lonely one—the unwanted one—and he says: You did it to me. Hungry for our love, and this is the hunger of our poor people. This is the hunger that you and I must find, it may be in our own home.

I never forget an opportunity I had in visiting a home where they had all these old parents of sons and daughters who had just put them in an institution and forgotten maybe. And I went there, and I saw in that home they had everything, beautiful things, but everybody was looking towards the door. And I did not see a single one with their smile on their face. And I turned to the Sister and I asked: How is that? How is it that the people they have everything here, why are they all looking towards the door, why are they not smiling? I am so used to see the smile on our people, even the dying one smile, and she said: This is nearly every day, they are expecting, they are hoping that a son or daughter will come to visit them. They are hurt because they are forgotten, and see—this is where love comes. That poverty comes right there in our own home, even neglect to love. Maybe in our own family we have somebody who is feeling lonely, who is feeling sick, who is feeling worried, and these are difficult days for everybody. Are we there, are we there to receive them, is the mother there to receive the child?

The poor people are very great people. They can teach us so many beautiful things. The other day one of them came to thank and said: You people who have vowed chastity you are the best people to teach us family planning. Because it is nothing more than self-control out of love for each other. And I think they said a beautiful sentence.

And these are people who maybe have nothing to eat, maybe they have not a home where to live, but they are great people. The poor are very wonderful people. One evening we went out and we picked up four people from the street. And one of them was in a most terrible condition—and I told the Sisters: You take care of the other three, I'll take care of this one that looked worse. So I did for her all that my love can do. I put her in bed, and there was such a beautiful smile on her face. She took hold of my hand, as she said one word only: Thank you—and she died.

I could not help but examine my conscience before her, and I asked what would I say if I was in her place? And my answer was very simple. I would have tried to draw a little attention to myself, I would have said I am hungry, that I am dying, I am cold, I am in pain, or something, but she gave me much more—she gave me her grateful love. And she died with a smile on her face. As that man whom we picked up from the drain, half eaten with worms, and we brought him to the home. I have lived like an animal in the street, but I am going to die like an angel, loved and cared for. And it was so wonderful to see the greatness of that man who could speak like that, who could die like that without blaming anybody, without cursing anybody, without comparing anything. Like an angel—this is the greatness of our people. And that is why we believe what Jesus had said: I was hungry—I was naked—I was homeless—I was unwanted, unloved, uncared for—and you did it to me.

I believe that we are not real social workers. We may be doing social work in the eyes of the people, but we are really contemplatives in the heart of the world. For we are touching the Body of Christ twenty fours hours. We have 24 hours in this presence, and so, you and I. You too try to bring that presence of God in your family, for the family that prays together stays together. And I think that we in our family don't need bombs and guns, to destroy to bring peace—just get together, love one another, bring that peace, that joy, that strength of presence of each other in the home. And we will be able to overcome all the evil that is in the world.

There is so much suffering, so much hatred, so much misery, and we with our prayer, with our sacrifice are beginning at home. Love begins at home, and it is not how much we do, but how much love we put in the action that we do. It is to God Almighty—how much we do it does not matter, because He is infinite, but how much love we put in that action. How much we do to Him in the person that we are serving.

Some time ago in Calcutta we had great difficulty in getting sugar, and I don't know how the word got around to the children, and a little boy of four years old, Hindu boy, went home and told his parents: I will not eat sugar for three days, I will give my sugar to Mother Teresa for her children. After three days his father and mother brought him to our home. I had never met them before, and this little one could scarcely pronounce my name, but he knew exactly what he had come to do. He knew that he wanted to share his love.

And this is why I have received such a lot of love from you all. From the time that I have come here I have simply been surrounded with love, and with real, real understanding love. It could feel as if everyone in India, everyone in Africa is somebody very special to you. And I felt quite at home I was telling Sister today. I feel in the Convent with the Sisters as if I am in Calcutta with my own Sisters. So completely at home here, right here.

And so here I am talking with you—I want you to find the poor here, right in your own home first. And begin love there. Be that good news to your own people. And find out about your next-door neighbour—do you know who they are?

To be able to do this, our Sisters, our lives have to be woven with prayer. They have to be woven with Christ to be able to understand, to be able to share. Because today there is so much suffering—and I feel that the passion of Christ is being relived all over again—are we there to share that passion, to share that suffering of people. Around the world, not only in the poor countries, but I found the poverty of the West so much more difficult to remove. When I pick up a person from the street, hungry, I give him a plate of rice, a piece of bread, I have satisfied. I have removed that hunger. But a person that is shut out, that feels unwanted, unloved, terrified, the person that has been thrown out from society—that poverty is so hurtable and so much, and I find that very difficult. Our Sisters are working amongst that kind of people in the West. So you must pray for us that we may be able to be that good news, but we cannot do that without you, you have to do that here in your country. You must come to know the poor, maybe our people here have material things, everything, but I think that if we all look into our own homes, how difficult we find it sometimes to smile at each, other, and that the smile is the beginning of love.

And so let us always meet each other with a smile, for the smile is the beginning of love, and once we begin to love each other naturally we want to do something. So you pray for our Sisters and for me and for our Brothers, and for our co-Workers that are around the world. That we may remain faithful to the gift of God, to love Him and serve Him in the poor together with you. What we have done we should not have been able to do if you did not share with your prayers, with your gifts, this continual giving. But I don't want you to give me from your abundance, I want that you give me until it hurts.

It is a gift of God to us to be able to share our love with others. And let it be as it was for Jesus. Let us love one another as he loved us. Let us love Him with undivided love. And the joy of loving Him and each other—let us give now—that Christmas is coming so close. Let us keep that joy of loving Jesus in our hearts. And share that joy with all that we come in touch with. And that radiating joy is real, for we have no reason not to be happy because we have no Christ with us. Christ in our hearts, Christ in the poor that we meet, Christ in the smile that we give and the smile that we receive. Let us make that one point: That no child will be unwanted, and also that we meet each other always with a smile, especially when it is difficult to smile.

I never forget some time ago about fourteen professors came from the United States from different universities. And they came to Calcutta to our house. Then we were talking about that they had been to the home for the dying. We have a home for the dying in Calcutta, where we have picked up more than 36,000 people only from the streets of Calcutta, and out of that big number more than 18,000 have died a beautiful death. They have just gone home to God; and they came to our house and we talked of love, of compassion, and then one of them asked me:

"Say, Mother, please tell us something that we will remember," and I said to them: *"Smile at each other, make time for each other in your family. Smile at each other."*

And I said: "Yes, I find it sometimes very difficult to smile at Jesus because he can be very demanding sometimes." This is really something true, and there is where love comes - when it is demanding, and yet we can give it to Him with joy.

Just as I have said today, I have said that if I don't go to Heaven for anything else I will be going to Heaven for all the publicity because it has purified me and sacrificed me and made me really ready to go to Heaven. I think that this is something, that we must live life beautifully: we have Jesus with us and He loves us.

If we could only remember that God loves me, and I have an opportunity to love others as he loves me, not in big things, but in small things with great love, then Norway becomes a nest of love. And how beautiful it will be that from here a centre for peace has been given. That from here the joy of life of the unborn child comes out. If you become a burning light in the world of peace, then really the Nobel Peace Prize is a gift of the Norwegian people.

God bless you.

The peace and the necessity of truth and reconciliation [22]

Desmond Tutu and others

The long apartheid era in South Africa saw horrific human rights abuses, and, alongside this, perhaps inevitably, widespread civil disorder and violence. To the outside world it seemed incredible that this state of continuing civil warfare and searing memories of horror could be followed by any move towards peace.

And yet, though never in human affairs, perfect, peace was in a measure, and not a small one, brought about.

The key, it seems, lay in the great Truth and Reconciliation Commission which worked in Cape Town from 1996 through a series of committees,. Its mandate was to bear witness to, record, and in some cases grant amnesty to, the perpetrators of crimes relating to human rights violations, as well as reparation and rehabilitation, to which a special committee (focused on here) was devoted.

It was an immense undertaking. Partly inspired by, though not identical with, the now forgotten Chilean Commission it was chaired by Archbishop Desmond Tutu, already, under apartheid, a charismatic worker for peace and reconciliation. He was assisted by a number of high-profile members, including Alex Boraine (deputy chairman), Sisi Khampepe, Wynand Malan, and Emma Mashinini, and, not least, the preparedness of both victims and perpetrators— themselves victims of the system—to speak truthfully and openly of what had happened.

Among the great gifts of this Commission not just to South Africa but to the world, are, in addition to its enormously imaginative and inspiring vision—its faith, in what could have been the direst and most abiding of human hatreds, in, ultimately, human goodness—its hugely practical and pragmatic input. No doubt no arrangements in this world are totally perfect —but the plans worked.

This is something that, in our zest for the search for peace, we sometimes forget. Prayer and faith are essential indeed. But by whose hands and thought is peace is, eventually, brought about? It may be through a large-scale Commission like this one. Or, as Sister Teresa reminds us, it may be though our small-great acts of love, a smile.

---

[22] *https://www.justice.gov.za/trc/reparations/summary.htm/*

Why reparation?
Thousands of people have been severely affected by the conflicts of the past. If we are to get over the past and build national unity and reconciliation, we must make sure that people who suffered gross human rights abuses are acknowledged by providing them with reparation. And subsequent links.

These measures cannot bring back the dead, or adequately compensate for pain and suffering, but they can improve the quality of life for victims of gross human rights violations and/or their dependants. The Committee on Reparation and Rehabilitation (the Committee) has developed reparation policy proposals.

What does reparation and rehabilitation mean?
Reparation and rehabilitation are words to describe what can be done to help victims overcome the damage that they suffered, to give them back their dignity and to make sure that these abuses do not happen again. Although this could include money, a financial payment is not the only form of reparation and rehabilitation that the Committee recommends. The Committee looked at individuals, communities and the nation as a whole when making recommendations to achieve reparation and rehabilitation.

The importance of reparation
There are several reasons for providing reparation. It is important that we know what these reasons are, so that we can understand why people will receive reparation.
back to top

The moral basis
- Victims of gross human rights abuses have the right to reparation and rehabilitation because of the many different types of losses they have suffered.
- Victims need to be compensated in some way, because the amnesty process means they lose the right to claim damages from perpetrators who are given amnesty.
- The present government has accepted that it must deal with the things the previous government did and that it must therefore take responsibility for reparation.

The legal basis
The Truth and Reconciliation Commission (TRC) was set up by an Act of Parliament, the Promotion of National Unity and Reconciliation Act. This Act says that the TRC must aim to:

Make proposals for measures that will give reparation to victims of human rights violations; and

Rehabilitate and give back the human and civil dignity of people who suffered human rights violations.

How did the Committee prepare its proposals?
The Committee collected information from many different places to make these proposals. Victims and survivors, people who made statements to the TRC, representatives of non-governmental organisations and community-based organisations, faith communities and academic institutions were all consulted by the Committee. Consultative workshops were held throughout the country. All the information collected by the Committee helped it to:

Find out the harm that was suffered;

Find out what the needs and expectations of victims are;

Work out ways to identify and help victims in immediate need; and

Make proposals for long term measures for reparation and rehabilitation.

Principles
A development-centred approach means that individuals and communities are helped to take control of their own lives. It is very important to provide individuals with knowledge and information about available resources and to help them use these resources in the way that benefits them most.

Proposals for reparation and rehabilitation need to be simple, efficient and fair. This means that the available resources will be used in a way which gives the most benefit to the people who receive them.

The services that are developed as a result of the proposals for reparation and rehabilitation should be sensitive to the religious and cultural beliefs and practices of the community.

Community-based services and delivery should be strengthened and expanded to have a lasting effect on communities.

Community resources which are developed should focus on local capacity building as well as the delivery of services.

The activities that come out of these proposals should aim to bring people together and to promote understanding, healing and reconciliation.

Symbolic reparation, legal and administrative measures
The Committee has made several proposals for symbolic reparation and other measures, which will help in legal and administrative matters. Symbolic reparation is to help communities remember the pain and the victories of the past. This could include setting aside a day for national

remembrance and reconciliation as well as the building of memorials and monuments.

The Committee has also proposed that steps are taken to help individuals to obtain death certificates, to sort out outstanding legal matters and to clear criminal records.

Symbolic reparation measures will restore the dignity of victims and survivors of gross human rights violations.

Victims identified through the TRC process, their families and communities at local, provincial and national levels will benefit from these measures. There will therefore be benefits which are for individuals only, as well as benefits which will be for the community and the nation.

Individual benefits
- Issuing of Death Certificates. Many people who made statements to the Commission said that they did not have death certificates for their relatives who had died or been killed.
- Exhumation, Reburials and Ceremonies. People who died during the conflicts were often buried in unmarked graves, and their relatives were not present at the burial. It is important for these bodies to be given a proper burial. The costs of the reburial and ceremonies will be taken from the IRG.
- Headstones and Tombstones. Relatives of people who died want their loved ones to have headstones or tombstones. The cost of these will come from the IRG.
- Declarations of Death. People who disappeared need to be formally declared dead.
- Clearing of Criminal Records. Many victims have criminal records because of their political activities. A criminal record may have serious consequences. It is therefore important that political activities are no longer seen as criminal.
- Resolving outstanding legal matters related to the violations. Legal processes which affect people now, and which are related directly to the gross human rights violations suffered by victims, need to be resolved.

Community benefits
- Renaming of streets and facilities. The renaming of streets and public buildings will help us remember individuals and events which are important to a community.
- Memorials/monuments. The building of memorials and monuments will commemorate the victories and the conflicts of the past, and will help to make sure that the abuses people have suffered do not happen again.
- Culturally appropriate ceremonies. The needs of the community must

be taken into account when ceremonies are held. It may be that ceremonies such as cleansing ceremonies are needed by communities.

National benefits
- Renaming of public facilities. Public buildings and structures need to be renamed in honour of individuals and past events.
- Monuments and memorials. National monuments and memorials should be built. These will remind people of the things that happened in the past, and help make sure that abuses do not happen again.
- A Day of Remembrance and Reconciliation. A national day of remembrance and reconciliation will remind people of the struggles and pain of the past, and help to bring about reconciliation, so that we are able to move forward from the past into the future.

Community rehabilitation
Community-based services and activities can promote the healing and recovery of individuals and communities affected by human rights violations. It is important that communities which have been affected by gross human rights abuses also benefit from reparation and rehabilitation measures. It is not enough to provide individual victims with resources and services, because this does not deal with the effects of gross human rights violations on the community as a whole.

These rehabilitation programmes should aim at developing and promoting reconciliation within communities
.

Health care
Young people have become used to using violence to resolve conflict. The youth were involved in violent activities to bring about political change. Now that political change has occurred, a programme should be developed that is aimed at bringing the youth back into education and work programmes. High schools, universities, technikons and sports bodies would be involved in the delivery of this programme.

Many people in South Africa have been driven from their homes by political conflict. People who have been forced to flee their homes often suffer emotional and psychological problems, as well as unemployment and difficulties caused by living in a strange place. A programme should be developed which will help resettle displaced communities.
- Victims and survivors of gross human rights violations have many physical and emotional needs. People with different skills, working at local clinics, are in the best position to help those who have suffered gross human rights violations.
- Perpetrators and their families also need to be brought back into normal

community life. Systems need to be set up to help individuals and their families come to terms with their violent past and to learn new ways of resolving conflict non-violently.

Mental health care
Support groups to assist victims and survivors should be established. These groups should be able to keep themselves going and be based within the community. Facilitators from the community would be trained in counselling. The support group method represents a cost-effective, accessible and non-threatening way in which people can receive counselling.

Victims of human rights abuses can be assisted in developing life skills. This will help them deal with the suffering they have experienced. Members of the community could be trained in a variety of skills so that they can assist victims of human rights abuses. These skills could include how to manage a crisis, how to be aware of what people have suffered, counselling skills for people using alcohol or drugs and counselling of people who have suffered gross human rights abuses.

A national strategy to train counsellors to help people who have suffered or committed gross human rights violations should be developed.

Family Based Therapy. The impact of gross human rights violations on the family is often underestimated. Health care workers should be able to help the family as a whole.

Education
Assistance for the Continuation of Studies:
The establishment of Community Colleges and Youth Centres is important and necessary so that the youth can become active members of their communities.
Adult Basic Educational Programmes (ABET) should be established to meet the needs of youth and adults who have lost education opportunities due to human rights abuses.
Demolished schools should be rebuilt as soon as possible.

Housing. Housing projects should be started in communities where the gross violation of human rights has resulted in the mass destruction of property or forced people to flee their homes.

Institutional reform
One of the tasks of the TRC is to make proposals on institutional, legislative and administrative measures to prevent human rights abuses from happening in the future. These proposals will include measures which will promote good governance, accountability and the prevention of human rights violations in civil society and the state.

The bitter legacy of war [23]
Victims and inspirers of the twenty-first century

It is not over. The pains of the early twentieth century are still with us. We do not learn.

Let us at the least listen. How can we not be touched by these poems from first-hand, intensely-felt, personal, tragedies? They come from the very front line of war and, for some, the dire experiences remain an enduring affliction (read the incredibly moving 'PTSD') for all their lives.

Afghanistan

A Soldier's Winter
The author watches as soldiers from all nations are daily taken on their final journey home from Kandahar. in Afghanistan."Nothing about war is peaceful; nothing about dying is graceful … but maybe in those last seconds, that last breath, that last blink….peace finds you."

What is this cold?
Where is this white?
Is this real, or just a fleeting moment of life, of my life?

I see no longer the greens and reds,
Where have the autumn leaves gone?
This must be the first signs of a new winter?

I see trees, I see sky, I see clouds,
All winter white,
Can I reach upward to touch the falling flake?
I try but never seem to connect,

And as I lay there staring at the sky
is my body cold ?
As I lay I hope I am not forgotten
But here I am alone.
I close my eyes and try to think of home.
Is this really happening to me?

---

[23] Taken from anonymous poetry in the internet on such sites as https://war-poetry.livejournal.com/668162.html/

This isn't real this is only a dream
I never have felt this way before, cold, weak and exposed,
but strangely at ease
With a tear I draw my parting breath
I'm looking down on my body below

I understand now this is winter.... this is my winter
                    ("Chris", a soldier in Kandahar, Afghanistan, 2009).

Syria

PTSD
Dedicated to those who will forever carry the anvil of trauma strapped to their backs.

The cell I live in is my mind, where I reside,
To those who will forever have the place I hide.
For me the past comes here to stay I fold away, I hide inside.
This cell is dank, it's walls sweat blood, its ceiling crushes from above.
The floor I see, the stench is sweat, this place is lacking warmth, and love.
I built this place with my own hand, the reason for to lock away
The light of day.
And darkness reigns in this foul place, the flashbacks come, the nightmares stay.
For whom the past comes round to call, my *sanga* hides me form the truth.
It shelters me from all that hate, its only covering roof.
And though to all I'm brash and bold, my outer skin seems hard and cold,
Reality is a different thing, I feel so weak, so used,
So Old.

I'll tell you how this came about, although I really have no doubt
That you already know
Because like me you have this room, the place to go, when you can shout.
It came about as I am weak, a person plagued by simple thoughts
That are not simple anymore, they squirm and toss, a hate, of sorts.
And when I close my eyes so tight, I see again the shattered forms
Of burning buildings, burning men, in bloody lightning storms
Of screaming children, arms and legs, just lying there, the dawn to find
Of shattered lives, of shattered minds, of shattered hopes from my own kind.
And so my cell protects me from this scene, but in itself provides a place
Where torture rules, the stinging whip, the tears of blood run down my face.

For in my mind, I built this place.
The bricks are moulded from my hate, are kiln-fired in the fire of life.
The mortar mixed from fear of death, and watered down with tears, and strife.
So course by course, as years went by, I built this cell
I learned to cry.

And when at last my time does come, when I lie down, to wilt and die
Then this fine shelter will collapse, fall over and be turned to dust.
For all my fears will go with me, my legacy of brick and rust.
My spirit then will fly so free, the past not there to trouble me.
I hope.

And so to you I say these things, to fellows who have lived like me
To you whose anguish rules your lives, fear not
For someday we'll be free.
    (Anonymous, from Syria – but it could be from any place of war, any century)

Ukraine [24]

Ukrainian authors, many of them displaced from their homes, give readings of their poetry which provoke powerful reflections on the importance of poetry, arts, and culture during the time of war.

The Spartan Boy

by Yuliya Musakovska

translated from the Ukrainian by Olena Jennings and the author

The war that you've been carrying
in your shirt pocket
gnawed a hole in you as if it were a fox.
Your heart keeps falling out.
I am sewing the hole shut,
firmly holding the edges together
with my numb, unbending fingers.
I hope it stays closed a little longer.

When the city falls asleep,
the black caterpillars of scars wake up.
And only death's head moths will emerge.
The city pours steam out of its nostrils
and sets its hills like horns.
You have a vision of your mates' faces
at the bottom of the lake —
a dark fairy tale from his childhood that came to life.
Although you were polite, respected elders, and were easily content.
Actually, there is no such thing as justice.
The scratched steel mug you never part with,
your superficial sleep, and fierce hate of fireworks.
What a lucky one, he could have lost so much more,
he's almost whole, they say.
You have chosen me because of my skillful, sensitive fingers.
I'm comfortable holding a needle with them.

---

[24] *https://www.apofenie.com/poetry/2022/5/15/yuliya-musakovska-poems/;*
https://munkschool.utoronto.ca/ceres/news/value-words-and-poetry-war-five-ukrainian-poets-showcase-their-experiences-through-their#:~:text=Five%20Ukrainian%20authors—Yuliya%20Musakovska,during%20the%20time%20of%20war.

A fox's muzzle is peering out of your pocket,
licking its lips, recalling what my bird of peace tasted like.

From President Volodymyr Zelensky's December 2020 address to US Congress after the Russian invasion of his beautiful country of Ukraine [25]

Dear members of the Congress, representatives of both parties who also visited Kyiv, esteemed congressmen and senators from both parties who will visit Ukraine, I am sure, in the future; dear representatives of diaspora, present in this chamber, and spread across the country; dear journalists, it's a great honor for me to be at the U.S. Congress and speak to you and all Americans.

Against all odds and doom-and-gloom scenarios, Ukraine didn't fall. Ukraine is alive and kicking. Thank you. And it gives me good reason to share with you our first, first joint victory: We defeated Russia in the battle for minds of the world. We have no fear, nor should anyone in the world have it. Ukrainians gained this victory, and it gives us courage which inspires the entire world.

Americans gained this victory, and that's why you have succeeded in uniting the global community to protect freedom and international law. Europeans gained this victory, and that's why Europe is now stronger and more independent than ever. The Russian tyranny has lost control over us. And it will never influence our minds again.

Yet, we have to do whatever it takes to ensure that countries of the Global South also gain such victory. I know one more, I think very important, thing: The Russians will stand a chance to be free only when they defeat the Kremlin in their minds. Yet, the battle continues, and we have to defeat the Kremlin on the battlefield, yes.

This battle is not only for the territory, for this or another part of Europe. The battle is not only for life, freedom and security of Ukrainians or any other nation which Russia attempts to conquer. This struggle will define in what world our children and grandchildren will live, and then their children and grandchildren.

It will define whether it will be a democracy of Ukrainians and for Americans — for all. This battle cannot be frozen or postponed. It cannot be ignored, hoping that the ocean or something else will provide a protection. From the United States to China, from Europe to Latin America, and from Africa to Australia, the world is too interconnected and

---

[25] *https://www.nytimes.com/2022/12/21/us/politics/zelensky-speech-transcript.html/*

interdependent to allow someone to stay aside and at the same time to feel safe when such a battle continues.

Our two nations are allies in this battle. And next year will be a turning point, I know it, the point when Ukrainian courage and American resolve must guarantee the future of our common freedom, the freedom of people who stand for their values.

Ladies and gentlemen — ladies and gentlemen, Americans, yesterday before coming here to Washington, D.C., I was at the front line in our Bakhmut. In our stronghold in the east of Ukraine, in the Donbas. The Russian military and mercenaries have been attacking Bakhmut nonstop since May. They have been attacking it day and night, but Bakhmut stands.

Last year — last year, 70,000 people lived here in Bakhmut, in this city, and now only few civilians stay. Every inch of that land is soaked in blood; roaring guns sound every hour. Trenches in the Donbas change hands several times a day in fierce combat, and even hand fighting. But the Ukrainian Donbas stands. …

Russia

X

Gaza 2023
The victims, the inspirers

In the early 2020s - today - we again, again, again, see the places of despair, amidst destruction, massacre, unyielding attack.

And yet - there was the released Israeli hostage who turned back to shake hands and shalom her captor in blessing and farewell - not this time perhaps, alas, but a gesture that might some time end a war ; the occasional smile that somehow cannot fail of a response, some response; the continuing human conviction, more than just an empty hope, that war is NOT the natural human order and that our children will have it better.

If only ...

A small great blessing[26]
Gaza News Team

Originally in Arabic, this reports a small but enduring act of generosity. Directed to practical help rather than "peace" as such, it might be said that it is in part in such acts of unselfishness that peace is created, and exists.

In December 2014, a Syrian refugee family with a father, mother and three children fled from Egypt to Gaza, hoping to find refuge and a fresh start. Fortunately, they were discovered by one of our Association members in Gaza who offered to let them live with him in his house. The father of this Association member also provided the Syrian family with some land to cultivate and grow their own food. Our Association member's father is a local farmer and a vegan, who follows the teachings of Supreme Master Ching Hai. He has 50 other farmer friends who also do the same.

The climate in this area is very dry, and the soil requires constant irrigation for crops to grow. Sadly, the local farmers' well was destroyed during the last conflict between Hamas and Israel in 2016. Like the other farmers who could no longer irrigate their land, the Syrian family was worried about their crops and their food supply.

On February 20, 2017, our Association members from Singapore provided financial support so the local well could be rebuilt, and to purchase a well

---

[26] Source: *The Supreme Master Ching Hai News Magazine*, at https://news.godsdirectcontact.net/lia-reports/fresh-start-syrian-refugee-families-gaza-160591/ (accessed May 2017).

water pump. The farmers can now irrigate their crops, and the well also provides drinking water for the Syrian refugee family as well as three more Syrian refugee families, including single mothers with children, who have now moved to the kind Palestinian farmer's land. On February 25, we delivered basic food necessities including wheat flour, lentils, rice, beans and vegetable oil to the families.

In March 2017, 10 more Syrian refugee families (a total of 46 people including children) moved to the farmland. The local farmers set up tents and accommodations for the new families who agreed to help on the farm, as more land needs to be cultivated. Also, a Palestinian furniture store donated many new mattresses for the Syrian families. At the local mosque, the Palestinian farmers prayed together with the Syrian families expressing gratitude to Allah for His grace and blessings.

By the end of April, the number of Syrian Refugees living on the farmland had risen to about 150, with three orphans being adopted by the family of one of our Palestinian Association members. In order to become more independent and self-sufficient, many Syrian refugees and Palestinian farmers have started to learn to make vegan bread and spinach pies from a local bakery owner. They plan to sell food in the market to buy flour and gasoline. Our Association members from Singapore kindly provided US$4,000 for this project. The farmland is becoming a happy home for the refugees. There have been three weddings between Palestinian young men and Syrian young women.

Our deep gratitude also for Allah's grace and blessings in providing the Syrian refugees a new home in Gaza. And our heartfelt appreciation to all the Palestinian farmers and the local people involved in welcoming and offering aid and assistance to the Syrian families. We pray that these families and all refugees will have a bright, prosperous and peaceful future (Gaza News, *The Supreme Master Ching Hai News Magazine*, at . https://news.godsdirectcontact.net/supreme-master-ching-hai-sends-congratulations-to-indias-new-prime-minister).

Peace is the beauty of life. It is sunshine. It is the smile of a child, the love of a mother, the joy of a father, the togetherness of a family. It is the advancement of man, the victory of a just cause, the triumph of truth (Menachem Begin, Prime Minister of Israel, 1977)

And the follow-up today?

"We raised our hands and carried white flags. Last night was very difficult. The sounds of explosions and gunfire was terrifying. The bulldozers created huge holes in the hospital yard and swept away some buildings".
(a message about trying to escape from a hospital in southern Gaza, November 2023; walking along rubble-strewn streets as gunfire rang out, how many of them didn't make it we do not know X@Rushdibbc/; https://www.bbc.co.uk/news/world-middle-east-67462615)

Hiroshima [27]

Barak Obama and Prime Minister Abe

Statements by the President of the USA and the Prime Minister of Japan at the Hiroshima PeaceMemorial on 17 May 2016, the 71st anniversary of the Hiroshima massacre.

PRESIDENT OBAMA:
 Seventy-one years ago, on a bright, cloudless morning, death fell from the sky and the world was changed. A flash of light and a wall of fire destroyed a city and demonstrated that mankind possessed the means to destroy itself.

Why do we come to this place, to Hiroshima? We come to ponder a terrible force unleashed in a not so distant past. We come to mourn the dead, including over 100,000 in Japanese men, women and children; thousands of Koreans; a dozen Americans held prisoner. Their souls speak to us. They ask us to look inward, to take stock of who we are and what we might become.

It is not the fact of war that sets Hiroshima apart. Artifacts tell us that violent conflict appeared with the very first man. Our early ancestors, having learned to make blades from flint and spears from wood, used these tools not just for hunting, but against their own kind. On every continent, the history of civilization is filled with war, whether driven by scarcity of grain or hunger for gold; compelled by nationalist fervour or religious zeal. Empires have risen and fallen. Peoples have been subjugated and liberated. And at each juncture, innocents have suffered, a countless toll, their names forgotten by time.

The World War that reached its brutal end in Hiroshima and Nagasaki was fought among the wealthiest and most powerful of nations. Their civilizations had given the world great cities and magnificent art. Their thinkers had advanced ideas of justice and harmony and truth. And yet, the war grew out of the same base instinct for domination or conquest that

---

[27] *https://www.nytimes.com/2016/05/28/world/asia/text-of-president-obamas-speech-in-hiroshima-japan.html#:~:text=Seventy-one years ago, on,to this place, to Hiroshima?/.*

had caused conflicts among the simplest tribes; an old pattern amplified by new capabilities and without new constraints. In the span of a few years, some 60 million people would die -- men, women, children no different than us, shot, beaten, marched, bombed, jailed, starved, gassed to death.

There are many sites around the world that chronicle this war -- memorials that tell stories of courage and heroism; graves and empty camps that echo of unspeakable depravity. Yet in the image of a mushroom cloud that rose into these skies, we are most starkly reminded of humanity's core contradiction; how the very spark that marks us as a species -- our thoughts, our imagination, our language, our tool-making, our ability to set ourselves apart from nature and bend it to our will -- those very things also give us the capacity for unmatched destruction.

How often does material advancement or social innovation blind us to this truth. How easily we learn to justify violence in the name of some higher cause. Every great religion promises a pathway to love and peace and righteousness, and yet no religion has been spared from believers who have claimed their faith as a license to kill. Nations arise, telling a story that binds people together in sacrifice and cooperation, allowing for remarkable feats, but those same stories have so often been used to oppress and dehumanize those who are different.

Science allows us to communicate across the seas and fly above the clouds; to cure disease and understand the cosmos. But those same discoveries can be turned into ever-more efficient killing machines.

The wars of the modern age teach this truth. Hiroshima teaches this truth. Technological progress without an equivalent progress in human institutions can doom us. The scientific revolution that led to the splitting of an atom requires a moral revolution, as well.

That is why we come to this place. We stand here, in the middle of this city, and force ourselves to imagine the moment the bomb fell. We force ourselves to feel the dread of children confused by what they see. We listen to a silent cry. We remember all the innocents killed across the arc of that terrible war, and the wars that came before, and the wars that would follow.

Mere words cannot give voice to such suffering, but we have a shared responsibility to look directly into the eye of history and ask what we must do differently to curb such suffering again. Someday the voices of the *hibakusha* will no longer be with us to bear witness. But the memory of the morning of August 6th, 1945 must never fade. That memory allows us to fight complacency. It fuels our moral imagination. It allows us to change.

And since that fateful day, we have made choices that give us hope. The United States and Japan forged not only an alliance, but a friendship that has won far more for our people than we could ever claim through war. The nations of Europe built a Union that replaced battlefields with bonds of commerce and democracy. Oppressed peoples and nations won liberation. An international community established institutions and treaties that worked to avoid war and aspire to restrict and roll back, and ultimately eliminate the existence of nuclear weapons.

Still, every act of aggression between nations; every act of terror and corruption and cruelty and oppression that we see around the world shows our work is never done. We may not be able to eliminate man's capacity to do evil, so nations—and the alliances that we've formed -- must possess the means to defend ourselves. But among those nations like my own that hold nuclear stockpiles, we must have the courage to escape the logic of fear, and pursue a world without them.

We may not realize this goal in my lifetime. But persistent effort can roll back the possibility of catastrophe. We can chart a course that leads to the destruction of these stockpiles. We can stop the spread to new nations, and secure deadly materials from fanatics.

And yet that is not enough. For we see around the world today how even the crudest rifles and barrel bombs can serve up violence on a terrible scale. We must change our mindset about war itself –- to prevent conflict through diplomacy, and strive to end conflicts after they've begun; to see our growing interdependence as a cause for peaceful cooperation and not violent competition; to define our nations not by our capacity to destroy, but by what we build.

And perhaps above all, we must reimagine our connection to one another as members of one human race. For this, too, is what makes our species unique. We're not bound by genetic code to repeat the mistakes of the past. We can learn. We can choose. We can tell our children a different story –- one that describes a common humanity; one that makes war less likely and cruelty less easily accepted.

We see these stories in the *hibakusha*—-the woman who forgave a pilot who flew the plane that dropped the atomic bomb, because she recognized that what she really hated was war itself; the man who sought out families of Americans killed here, because he believed their loss was equal to his own.

My own nation's story began with simple words: All men are created equal, and endowed by our Creator with certain unalienable rights, including life, liberty and the pursuit of happiness. Realizing that ideal has never been easy, even within our own borders, even among our own citizens.

But staying true to that story is worth the effort. It is an ideal to be strived for; an ideal that extends across continents, and across oceans. The irreducible worth of every person, the insistence that every life is precious; the radical and necessary notion that we are part of a single human family—that is the story that we all must tell.

That is why we come to Hiroshima. So that we might think of people we love -- the first smile from our children in the morning; the gentle touch from a spouse over the kitchen table; the comforting embrace of a parent -- we can think of those things and know that those same precious moments took place here seventy-one years ago. Those who died—they are like us. Ordinary people understand this, I think. They do not want more war. They would rather that the wonders of science be focused on improving life, and not eliminating it.

When the choices made by nations, when the choices made by leaders reflect this simple wisdom, then the lesson of Hiroshima is done.

The world was forever changed here. But today, the children of this city will go through their day in peace. What a precious thing that is. It is worth protecting, and then extending to every child. That is the future we can choose—a future in which Hiroshima and Nagasaki are known not as the dawn of atomic warfare, but as the start of our own moral awakening. (Applause.)

PRIME MINISTER ABE:
(as translated) Last year, at the 70th anniversary of the end of war, I visited the United States and made a speech as Prime Minister of Japan at a joint meeting of the U.S. Congress. That war deprived many American youngsters of their dreams and futures. Reflecting upon such harsh history, I offered my eternal condolences to all the American souls that were lost during World War II. I expressed gratitude and respect for all the people in both Japan and the United States who have been committed to reconciliation for the past 70 years.

Seventy years later, enemies who fought each other so fiercely have become friends, bonded in spirit, and have become allies, bound in trust and friendship, deep between us. The Japan-U.S. alliance, which came into the world this way, has to be an alliance of hope for the world.

So I appealed in the speech. One year has passed since then. This time, President Obama, for the first time as leader of the United States, paid a visit to Hiroshima, the city which suffered the atomic bombing. U.S. President witnessing the reality of atomic bombings and renewing his determination for a world free of nuclear weapons--this gives great hope to people all around the world who have never given up their hope for a world without nuclear weapons.

I would like to give a whole-hearted welcome to this historic visit, which had been awaited not only by the people of Hiroshima, but also by all the Japanese people. I express my sincere respect to the decision and courage of President Obama. With his decision and courage, we are opening a new chapter to the reconciliation of Japan and the United States, and in our history of trust and friendship.

A few minutes ago, together, I and President Obama offered our deepest condolences for all those who lost their lives during World War II and also by the atomic bombings. Seventy-one years ago in Hiroshima and in Nagasaki, a great number of innocent citizens' lives were cost by a single atomic bomb without mercy. Many children and many citizens perished. Each one of them had his or her life dream and beloved family. When I reflect on this sheer fact, I cannot help but feel painful grief.

Even today, there are victims who are still suffering unbearably from the bombings. Feeling of those who went through unimaginable tragic experiences, indeed, in this city 71 years ago -- it is unspeakable. In their minds, various feelings must have come and gone -- that of those, this must be in common: That any place in the world this tragedy must not be repeated again.

It is the responsibility of us who live in the present to firmly inherit these deep feelings. We are determined to realize a world free of nuclear weapons. No matter how long and how difficult the road will be, it is the responsibility of us who live in the present to continue to make efforts.

Children who were born on that unforgettable day lit the light believing in permanent peace. To make every effort for the peace and prosperity in the world, vowing for this light-- his is the responsibility of us all who live in the present. We will definitely fulfill our responsibility. Together, Japan and the United States will become a light for hope, for the people in the world.
 Standing in this city, I am firmly determined, together with President Obama. This is the only way to respond to the feelings of the countless spirits--victims of the atomic bombs in Hiroshima and Nagasaki. I am convinced of this.

Prayer for peace
Unknown author

An anonymous prayer displayed in New Zealand's Christchurch cathedral: the "transitional", deeply charismatic and awesomely soaring, building of cardboard raised in hope and commitment after the devastating earthquake of 2011.

As well as the displayed prayer, in the chancel there were the small, modestly inscribed, words

> *"Let this be a sign of*
> *letting go old sorrows*
> *hope for tomorrow*
> *gratitude for today".*

God of many names
    Lover of all peoples;
    We pray for peace in our nations
    And in our world.

We pray for all who have the awesome responsibility of power and decision-making.

We pray for the innocent victims of violence and war.

Lead us and all the peoples of the world
    From death to life, from falsehood to truth.
    Lead us from despair to hope, from fear to trust.
    Lead us from hate to love, from war to peace.

    Let peace with justice fill our hearts
                      our world
          our universe.

A FEW PEACE SYMBOLS

Peace is expressed not just in words and music, but also, and essentially, in people's actions and in beautiful, meaningful visual symbols.

A few examples, among the multitude of widely-known, beautiful, and emotionally stirring, peace symbols are, in the west, the dove, in Japan the crane, in Maori tradition the spiral and unfurling fern - and many many others, in fact all through the "oekoumenee" - the ancient Greek word for our lovely inhabited world (for some others see (and even then not comprehensive, https://unsplash.com/s/photos/peace-sign/; https://www.britannica.com/story/where-did-the-peace-sign-come-from/; https://en.wikipedia.org/wiki/Peace_symbols/)

Māori unwinding fern symbol of unfolding life and peace

141

142

The broken rifle,
    symbol of
The War Resisters' International

And the people who make it happen

*****

FURTHER THOUGHTS

Sadako and the Thousand Paper Cranes, 1994.

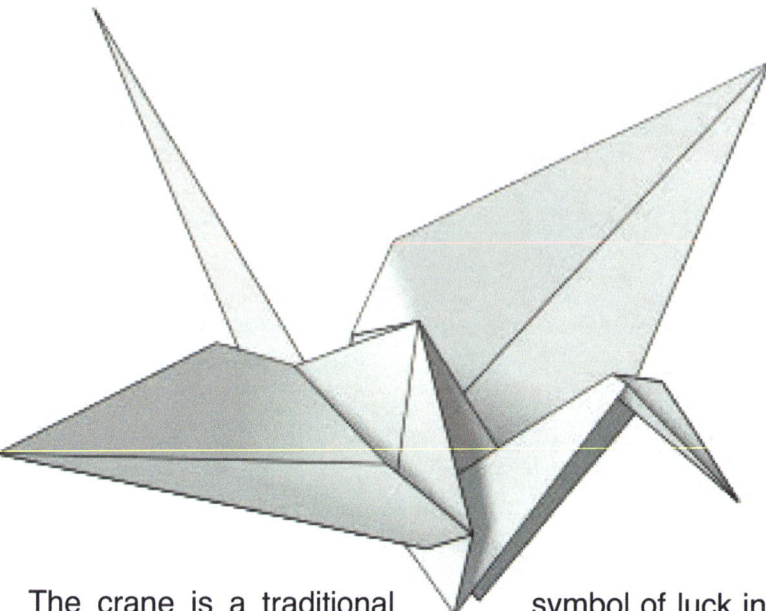

The crane is a traditional symbol of luck in Japan and became a peace symbol from the story of Sadako Sasaki (1943–1955), a girl who died as a result of the atomic bomb exploding over Hiroshima in 1945. In the last stages of her illness she started folding paper cranes, inspired by the Japanese saying that one who folded a thousand origami cranes was granted a wish. She is remembered every 6 August, an annual peace day for people all over Japan.

Evelyn Glennie, *Listen World*, 2019.

About music and percussion, by the premier (profoundly deaf) world solo percussionist. The book argues that if we learn to listen more truly, music can bring harmony and peace to the world.

Steve Killelea, *Peace in an Age of Chaos*, 2020

A personal journey to measure and understand peace by the creator of the Global Peace Index and founder of world-renowned think tank, the Institute for Economics and Peace. It explores the practical application of this

146

work, and offers a new way of conceptualising how to create a peaceful world.

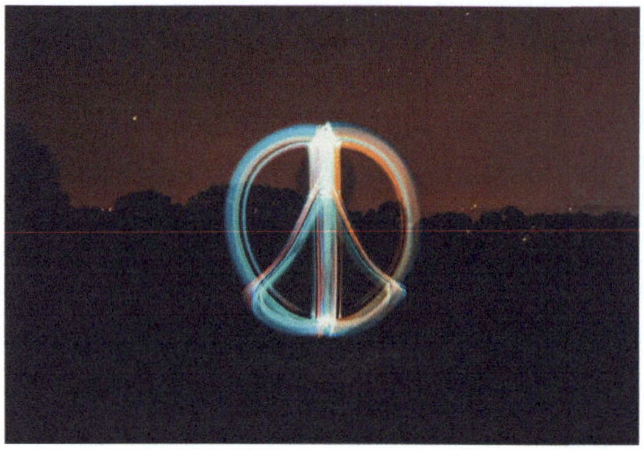

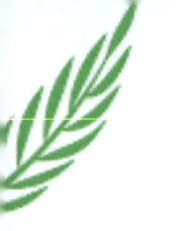